Introduction

The first volume of Kittiwake's La gave an inkling of how many lak volume I have tried to include some o as some that are blatantly obvious. The ability and ages.

On many of these walks you will probably never meet another walker. Only the sheep will be your companions. Oh, and the odd bird, rabbit, hare, fox or deer will be watching your every move. Even much rarer animals can be seen, such as otters and pine martens.

Lakes are quintessential features of mountain scenery and often give a sense of well being. Some, high in the mountains, need the necessary skills to reach them, especially in bad weather. So don't visit these when they are shrouded in clinging mist and driving drizzle. Or, IF you have the requisite mountain skills, perhaps you should. It is when they suddenly appear out of nowhere that their mystical qualities are at their highest.

Needless to say proper walking clothing is needed as there will be rough and boggy ground on some the walks. Do not rely on your mobile phone to raise the alarm if you have an accident – phone signals are often non-existent in the hills. Most of the walks are easy to follow but a good sense of direction is required on some when the paths disappear. Be sure you know what to do if the mist descends. The two most demanding walks are the circuit of Llyn Trawsfynnydd (**Walk 17**) and Llyn Cwm y Foel, Llynnau Diffwys & Llyn Croesor (**Walk 9**), UNLESS you take the alternative suggested in **Walk 5** to climb Snowdon.

This volume has walks from the Carneddau in the north of Snowdonia all the way down to Llyn Clywedog near Llanidloes, just beyond the edge of the Snowdonia National Park. Some lake names will be familiar to regular walkers but some may just conjure up the feeling of 'well, where the heck is that one'. Some of the walks are ideally suited for taking along a picnic with you – Llyn Mair and Llyn Clywedog are examples.

It is important to remember that swimming in reservoirs is not allowed or indeed advisable. The water in the high mountain lakes is usually bitterly cold and very deep. Don't go in, even after a hot sweaty day.

If you find any changes that need to be made to this guide please contact me via the publisher (editor@kittiwake-books.com). I hope you enjoy the walks in this second guide as much as you did in the first.

WALK I
MELYNLLYN & DULYN

DESCRIPTION A fine, unfrequented 6½ mile walk in a remote area of the Carneddau. There are wild ponies here. The outward walk follows a good track whilst the return walk has some boggy sections. Allow 3 hours. Afon Carreg-wen may be impassable after wet weather

START From the car parking area at the end of the driveable road.

DIRECTIONS From Betws y Coed drive along the A470 to Llanrwst. Turn left over the bridge on to the B5106. Follow this road through Trefriw and Dolgarrog to Tal-y-Bont. Turn left 100 yards before the Y Bedol inn. Follow this initially steep and narrow road, ignoring the left turning after 1¼ miles, through three gates for 1¼ miles to the car parking area on your right.

1 Climb over the waymarked ladder stile to the right of the car park and follow the wide track up to and over the ladder stile to the right of a gate. Follow the track uphill, ignoring the right hand one, and pass through two small rock outcrops followed by some ruins on your right. Keep walking up the track – there is a good view of Llyn Eigiau to your left. Continue on the track and go over a ladder stile to the right of a gate and to and over the next one. The track gradually rises with the valley of Pant y Griafolen on your right and a glimpse of Dulyn is seen to your right. The track levels and continues to where it bears right to pass a ruin on your left.

2 Go over the sleeper bridge where you will notice the housing for a water wheel and slate workings high up on the mountain. The track ends at Melynllyn – *a peaceful lake situated below the steep slope of Foel Fras.* Cross the footbridge over the outlet stream and follow the obvious path by the left hand side of the stream until it bears away from it. The path descends steeply below a low angled crag to where it rounds a corner. Here there is a dramatic view of *Dulyn below the brooding cliffs.* When the path reaches to what appears to be stone embankment bear right. Cross over the pipe to view the full extent of the lake. *You now notice that the 'stone embankment' is a covering for a discharge pipe, creating a waterfall.*

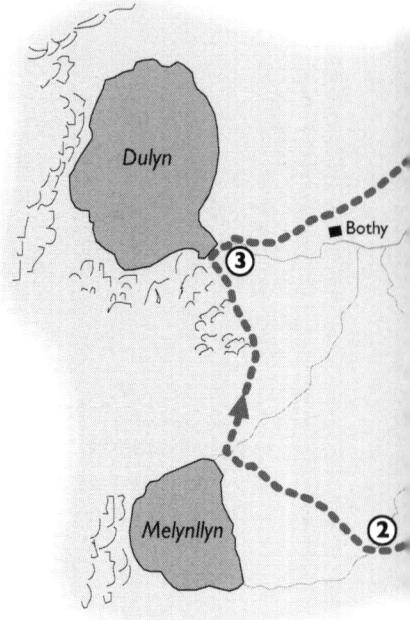

3 The path continues to the lake outlet. Cross this and bear right to the obvious house. *This is a bothy belonging to the Mountain Bothies Association. Please respect this property.* The path continues above the bothy and becomes very boggy. Continue to reach and go over a rickety metal ladder stile crossing a fence. The path still continues damply to climb over another rickety ladder stile. More swampy ground is crossed to reach the Afon Garreg-wen. Cross this – although it may be impassable after wet weather. The path continues and bears right over more boggy ground to another stile. Climb over this to reach a track by a small hut on your left.

WALK 1

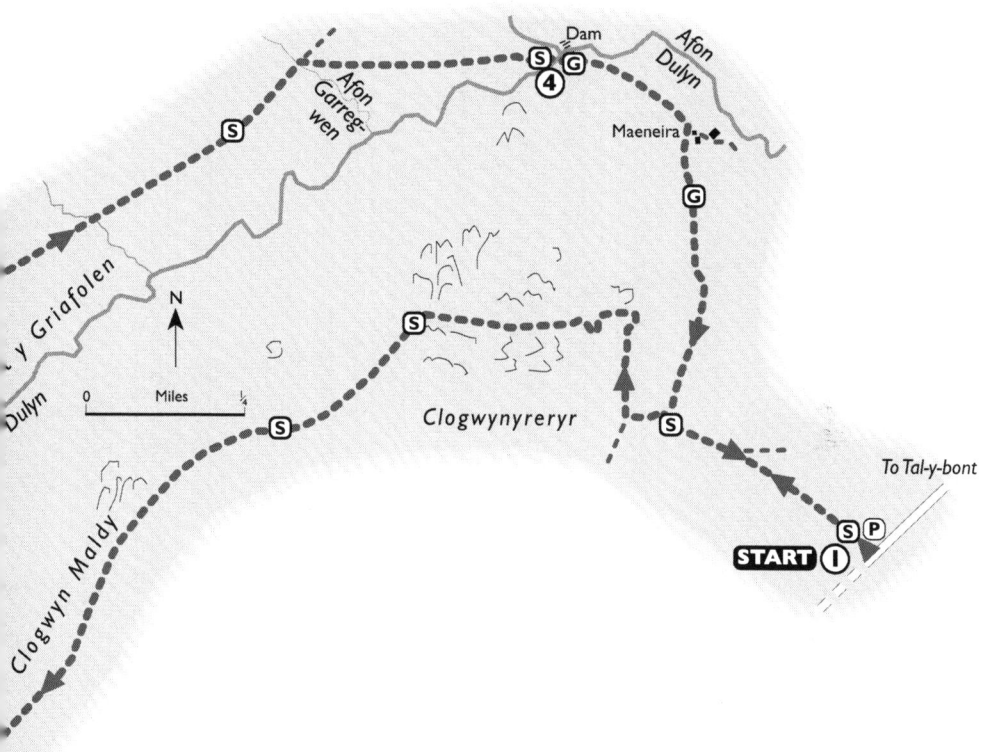

4 Follow this short section of track to the dam. DO NOT cross this but go straight ahead through a waymarked gate and follow the track bearing right. Continue up the track to and through a gate. The track continues up and through another gate. Keep walking up to join the track of your outward walk close to the two rock outcrops. Turn left down the track back to your car.

Dulyn *translates as Black Lake. Although only covering 33 acres it is about 185 feet deep. Apart from being a site of several small aeroplane crashes the area is full of superstition. The dam was built in 1881. It provides, along with Melynllyn, water for Llandudno. The river flowing from Dulyn is the Afon Dulyn.*

WALK 2
RHAEADR OGWEN, LLYN OGWEN & FFYNNON LLOER

DESCRIPTION If going to Ffynnon Lloer this is a fine, wild 5½ mile scenic walk into the dramatic confines of Cwm Lloer. However, the easier version is still a lovely 3 mile walk that has some great views. The waterfall is also a fine sight especially after heavy rain and is well worth the few extra minutes to view. Allow 3 hours for the walk into Cwm Lloer and 1½ hours for the easier option.

START From the Snowdonia National Park car park at Ogwen Cottage.

DIRECTIONS From Betws y Coed drive along the A5 towards Bangor. Drive through Capel Curig and continue below Tryfan to reach the sign at the far end of Llyn Ogwen indicating where you turn left into the car park. There is also a sign for the Youth Hostel. A small fee is payable but there are toilets, an information service and a snack bar here.

1 From the car park return to the A5 and walk down the road away from the lake to the second gate on your left. Go through this to admire the wonderful waterfall. Return to the road and cross over to a stile by the side of a finger post. Go over the stile. Descend to the river and look at the very old – supposedly Roman – bridge below the modern road bridge. From the stile follow the rocky path to the left of the river with care. Go down a 3 yards step and then up 3 yards. Bear right around boulders to reach the low dam at the end of the lake.

2 Follow the edge of the lake past a WW2 pill box and continue to go over a ladder stile. The path climbs easily up and away from the lake to continue through a gap in the wall. Keep following the path past a cairn to your right. Occasional cairns guide you through the next section across some wet ground to reach and climb over another ladder stile. More boggy ground – in wet weather – reaches some stepping stones and a marker post. Follow the path bearing left to another ladder stile. Climb over this and cross a footbridge immediately after. Bear left over a small clapper bridge and walk up to a marker post. Continue past more marker posts to the next ladder stile. If not going to Cwm Lloer continue as in 4 below.

3 If you do decide to go up to Cwm Lloer this where you start. Instead of going over the stile follow the constructed path keeping to the right of the Afon Lloer following the line of marker posts. At a level section there are several branches of the river Cross to the right and then all the way back left to the far side of them picking your crossing places carefully. Continue up the path past occasional marker posts to climb over a ladder stile at the wall. Continue into Cwm Lloer and Ffynnon Lloer. Return to the stile where you started.

4 Climb over the stile and turn right down the constructed path to a track. Turn right along it and go over a ladder stile to the right of a cattle grid. Continue past Glan Dena, a climbing club hut belonging to the Midland association of Mountaineers, to the A5. Turn right and follow this back to your car. Although next to the road it is not unpleasant and the views are superb.

About the author, Des Marshall

Des has had a lifelong interest in mountaineering, climbing, walking, canyoning and caving. As well as being an advisor, trainer and assessor in outdoor activities, he has undertaken many expeditions worldwide but now focuses more on local excursions. After moving away a couple of years ago, the lure of the plethora of exciting walking and climbing became too much and he has now returned to Wales.

WALK 2

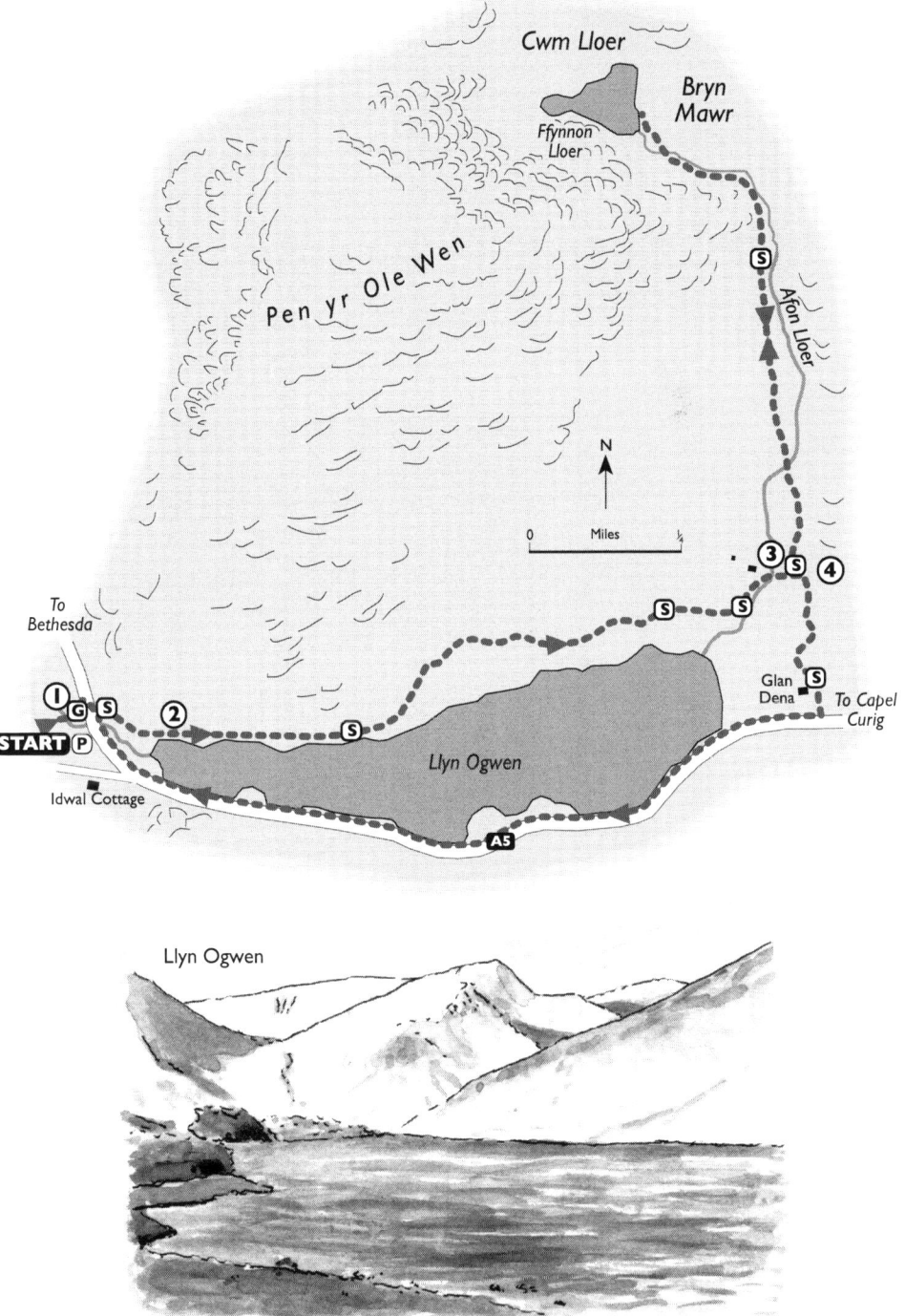

Llyn Ogwen

1 From the car park follow the path to the left of the buildings that house the information office and facilities up to and through a gate. Cross the footbridge immediately after and continue up the constructed path to where it splits and the constructed path bears right. Take the left smaller branch and follow this rougher path. It gets steeper as height is gained. As the cascades of the Nant Bochlwyd are approached the path is very steep but without difficulty. At the top of the cascades the path loses itself in boulders but just continue straight ahead to the lake. A fine place.

2 From the lake walk to your right on a faint path that quickly becomes more pronounced and is easily followed. It rises gradually away from the lake to reach the top of a rise where the path splits. The left hand one ascends the Gribin Facet. Follow the right hand path over a very low wall and continue over the shoulder of the Gribin Facet to the top of a wide, steep and stony gully. Descend this with care to the easier lower grassy slopes leading down to the path alongside Llyn Idwal. Turn right and go through a gate. Continue on the constructed path to where it veers right away from the end of the lake to continue down to Ogwen Cottage and your car.

WALK 3
LLYN BOCHLWYD & LLYN IDWAL

DESCRIPTION This good mountain walk of 2¼ miles reaches the fine Llyn Bochlwyd nestling below the beetling and high cliffs of Glyder Fach, home to some very fine rock climbs. The walk continues by crossing over the shoulder of the Gribin Facet to descend a steep gully and grassy slope to reach the shore of Llyn Idwal. An easy walk takes you back from here to Ogwen Cottage. There is a fine sense of being high in the mountains on the walk away from Llyn Bochlwyd. Allow 1¾ hours.

START From the Snowdonia National Park car park at Ogwen Cottage.

DIRECTIONS From Betws y Coed drive along the A5 towards Bangor. Drive through Capel Curig and continue below Tryfan to reach the sign at the far end of Llyn Ogwen indicating where you turn left into the car park. There is also a sign for the Youth Hostel. A small fee is payable but there are toilets, an information service and a snack bar here.

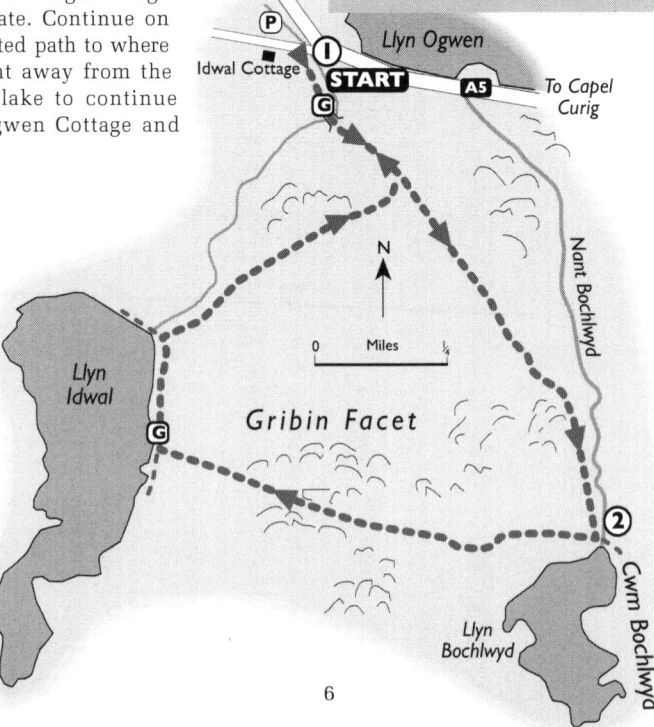

WALKS 3 & 4

WALK 4
LLYN CWMFFYNNON

DESCRIPTION The walk to this scenic lake has the feeling, once you are away from the bustle of Pen y Pass, of being remote yet it is only a very short distance away. It is ideally suited as an extension to Walk 5 (you then only pay the car parking fee once) or you may like just to go for a picnic to this lovely spot. Allow half an hour, or longer if picnicking, for the half a mile there and back walk.

START From the Snowdonia National Park car park at Pen y Pass.

DIRECTIONS From Betws y Coed drive along the A5 towards Bangor. In Capel Curig turn left immediately before the Pinnacle Café on to the A4086, where there is a grassy triangle. Follow this road, passing Plas y Brenin the National Outdoor Centre, to the Pen y Gwryd. Turn right here still on the A4086 and continue to the top of the pass by the youth hostel on the right and the car park on your left. Park here where a fee is payable but there are toilets and a café. On summer mornings this car park is usually full by 08.00! If the car park is full use the Park and Ride service.

Walk out of the car park and cross the road to the Youth Hostel. Go through the gate immediately to the left of the building and walk up to a metal kissing gate 20 yards further. This leads to the open hillside and, although quite steep, the path quickly reaches a storage tank with a metal grid over the top of it. There are some pretty bands of quartz here. Continue another 50 yards to where a cairn is seen to your right. Go right here and follow the path to the lake. Enjoy your surroundings and then return by the same route to the car park.

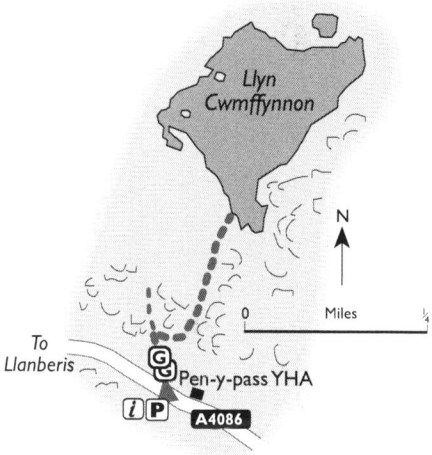

Llyn Idwal.

WALK 5
GLASLYN, LLYN LLYDAW & LLYN TERYN

DESCRIPTION This 6 mile mountain walk goes through some great mountain scenery, especially Glaslyn, having the massive summit cliffs of Snowdon towering behind it and of course Llyn Llydaw with Lliwedd beyond. The walk is very easy to follow although there are some rougher sections. Allow 3½ hours.

START From the Snowdonia National Park car park at Pen y Pass.

DIRECTIONS From Betws y Coed drive along the A5 towards Bangor. In Capel Curig turn left immediately before the Pinnacle Café on to the A4086 where there is a grassy triangle. Follow this road, passing Plas y Brenin the National Outdoor Centre, to the Pen y Gwryd. Turn right here still on the A4086 and continue to the top of the pass by the youth hostel on the right and the car park on your left. Park here where a fee is payable but there are toilets and a café. On summer mornings this car park is usually full by 08.00! If the car park is full use the Park and Ride service.

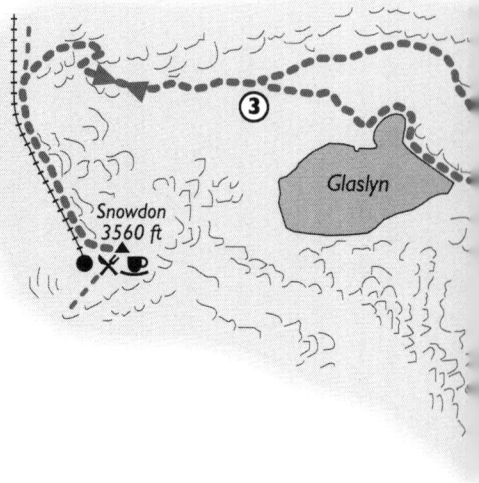

1 From the car park take the tarmac path from the highest corner where there is also a sign for the PYG track. At the end of the tarmac an easily followed constructed path continues to Bwlch y Moch below the extremely steep slopes of Crib Goch. On the way pause to look down Llanberis Pass to view Llyn Peris and beyond that Llyn Padarn. Behind you there is Pen y Pass and Llyn Cwnffynnon. At the bwlch continue to twin stiles from which you have a fine overlook of Llyn Llydaw and across to Lliwedd.

2 Climb over one of these and continue along a level section to where it begins to climb steadily on a constructed path. Glaslyn suddenly appears. Continue up on a rougher path to some cairns and a very fine view down to Glaslyn and the massive craggy bulk of Snowdon rising above it. Keep following the path high above Glaslyn to the junction with the Miner's Track. Here you have two options: **1** – The summit of Snowdon is not far away so continue up steeply to the finger stone and the nearby railway. Continue up the path on the left of the railway to the summer cafe and summit terminus of the railway. Climb up the steps to reach the summit of the highest point in Wales and England. Return to the junction of the PYG and Miner's Tracks.

3 From the junction of the PYG and Miner's Tracks turn left and follow the steep rough path down to the shore of Glaslyn reaching it a finger stone by a track. Turn left along the track around the edge of the lake. At the end of the lake the path descends gradually to Llyn Llydaw. Follow the track around the lake passing

WALK 5

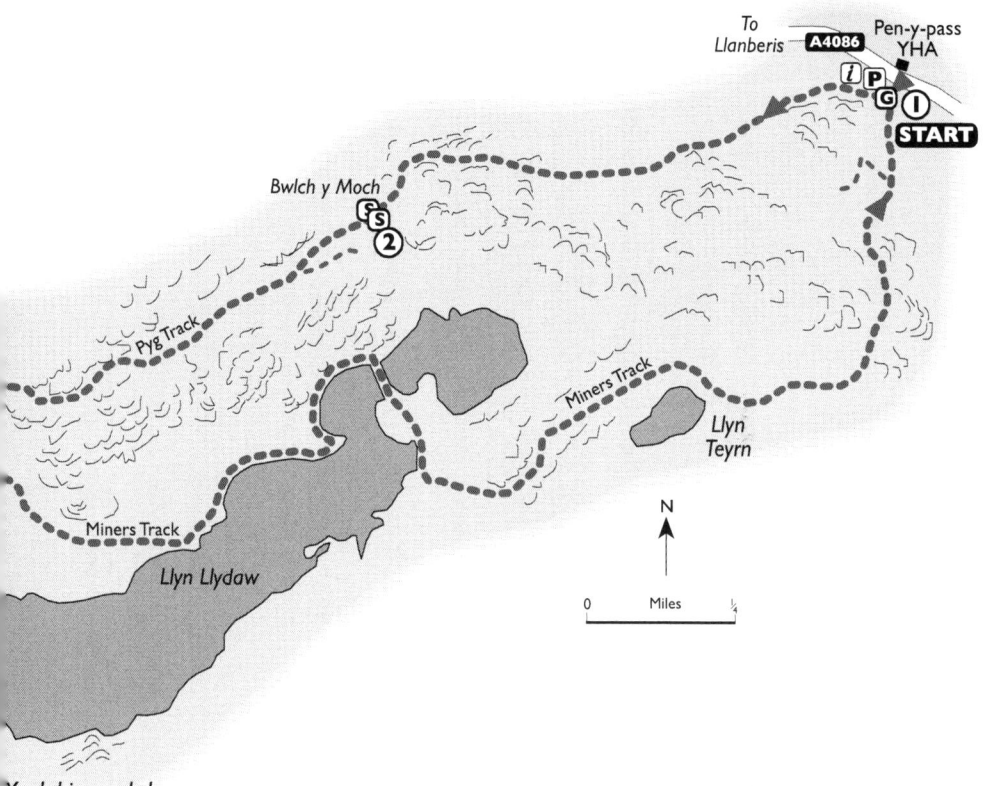

Y Lliwedd

the stark remains of the crushing mill for the Britannia Copper Mine. Continue to the causeway and cross it. At the far side a well maintained track is followed easily down to Llyn Teyrn and then slightly up and down again to the car park at Pen y Pass and your car

*T*he **Miner's Track** was built to serve the Britannia Copper Mine, although the current track does not follow the original. Originally copper was taken eastwards over the mountain to Llyn Cwellyn before being transported to Caernarfon. Some ten years or so later the road from Llanberis to Pen y Gwryd was built enabling this easier access to be used to transport the ore.

*T*he **mine** was first mentioned around 1800 and was worked intermittently but somewhat unsuccessfully for over a hundred years with the most well known, The Britannia Copper Mine Ltd, starting in 1898. The final company to work the mines was the Penypass Copper Company, which started mining in 1915, but all work ceased in 1916 when the mine closed. There were eight levels.

WALK 6
LLYN GWYNANT

DESCRIPTION This is a lovely 3½ mile walk to a very pretty and scenic lake, Even though you walk along the road towards the end this does not detract from the experience as the pavement follows the lake for much of the way. The path is easy to follow. Allow 1¾ hours.

START From the car parking just after entering Nantgwynant.

DIRECTIONS From Betws y Coed drive along the A5 towards Bangor. In Capel Curig turn left immediately before the Pinnacle Café on to the A4086 where there is a grassy triangle. Follow this road, passing Plas y Brenin the National Outdoor Centre, to the Pen y Gwryd. Continue straight ahead here and descend the twisting A498 to Llyn Gwynant. Continue past the lake to the Nantgwynant and 40 mph sign. Turn left into the signed car parking area 200 yards beyond. There is a house immediately beyond the parking area.

1 Walk back up the road towards the lake for 300 yards to a gate on your left by a finger post. Go through this and over a stile 30 yards further. Pass through a gate 100 yards further on again to reach and cross a very fine footbridge. Go through the gate on the far side and turn right to reach a track. Turn right along it to a ruin on your left hand side, just before the house at the end of the track. Turn left at the ruin and walk up to a junction with a rough track. Turn right and go through a gap in the wall. Continue up the path that goes through a small abandoned mine working to where the path meets a wall on your right. At the top of the rise the path descends and continues along to a ladder stile.

2 Climb over this and follow the path over a log footbridge through the wood above Llyn Gwynant. Cross another footbridge and climb up to the top of a rocky bluff, Penmaen-brith, but take CARE, there is a long drop to your right into the lake! Just beyond the summit there is a rock outcrop and a splendid, small, flat, grassy belvedere, an ideal place for sandwiches. There are superb views of the lake too. The path descends steeply from here and levels before crossing two footbridges. Continue along and then gradually down to climb over a ladder stile. Follow the path next to the wall on your right and continue to go through a gate. The path goes below Clogwyn y Wenallt, the fine rock climber's crag high up to your left, to reach a footbridge over the Afon Glaslyn.

3 Walk through the gate and cross the footbridge. Turn right by the side of the river and bear slightly left to some white-topped posts at the edge of a parking/turning area at the end of a track. Walk across this to a track junction and bear left to a solitary white-topped post between two small wooded enclosures. Walk ahead to the lake shore. Turn left along this to pass a seat on your left just before reaching a ladder stile. Climb over this and follow the path up with a great view down the lake. Continue through a short section of high gorse bushes. The path descends to the lake shore again. Follow this. At times of high water levels this could be a wade in shallow water! Continue to go over a ladder stile a short distance from the road. Turn right and follow the pavement alongside the lake back to your car.

The area has been used as a film set with two blockbusters being made in the area. The most recent one – filmed in 2003 – was 'Lara Croft Tomb Raider: The Cradle of Life'. Llyn Gwynant was one of many sites used world-wide whilst the film was being made. However, one of the greatest films of all time was 'The Inn of

To Beddgelert

the Sixth Happiness' filmed here in 1957 and released in 1958. Not being allowed to film on Formosa, Mark Robson, the Director, made the film here because the area is very similar to Chinese scenery. Several other locations throughout North Wales were used, such as Beddgelert, Ogwen (Tryfan), Sygun Copper Mine, Capel Curig and Morfa Bychan to name a few. The film, based on an Alan Burgess book 'The Small Woman', tells the true story of Gladys Aylward, played by Ingrid Bergman, a British maid turned missionary during the Second Sino-Japanese war in the 1930s. Other stars were Curt Jurgens and Robert Donat, who sadly died after falling ill towards the end of filming.

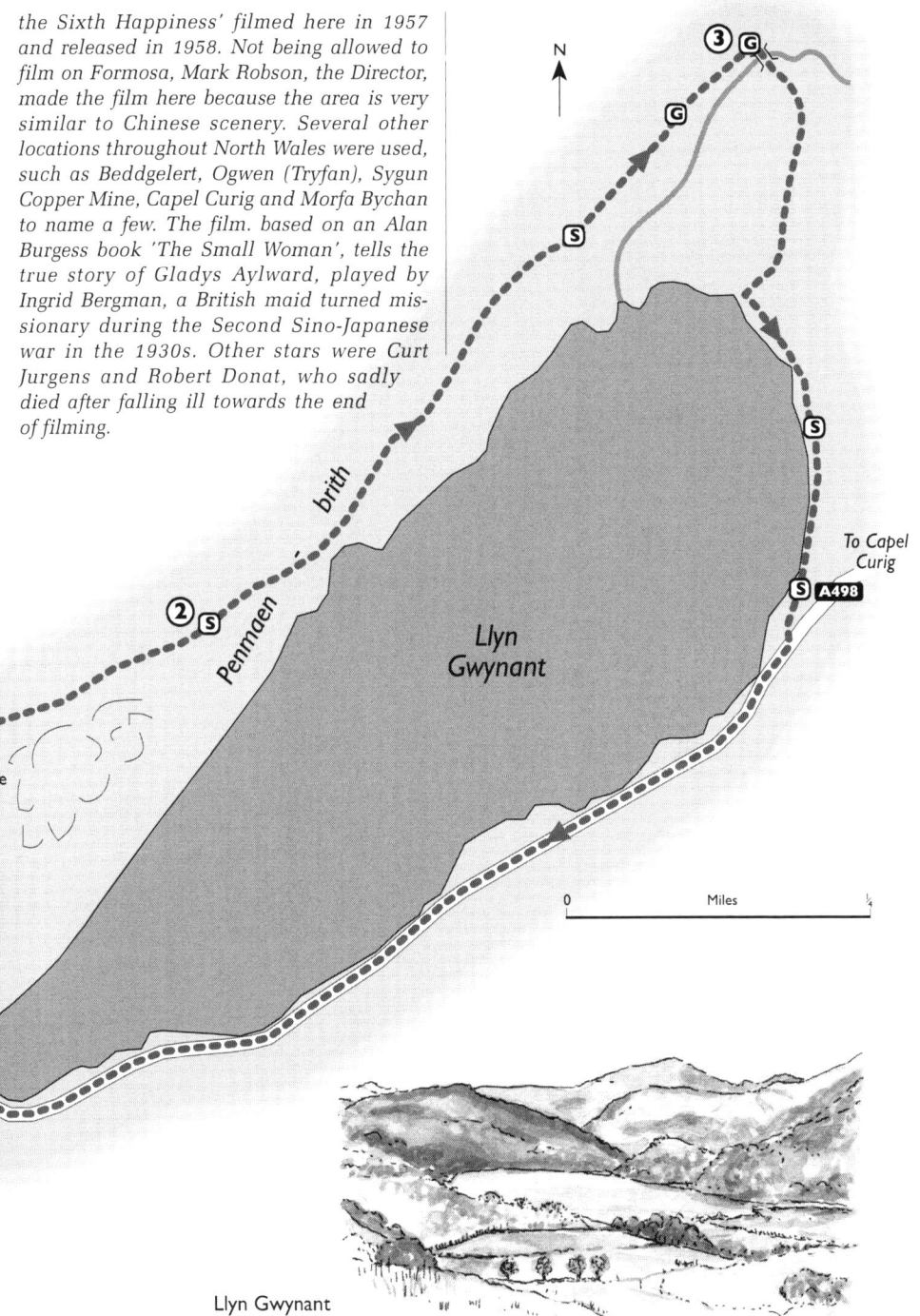

Llyn Gwynant

WALK 7
LLYN DINAS

DESCRIPTION Although this walk is only 1½ miles long it is very pretty and scenic, ideally suited for a short evening or with young children. The path is easy to follow but can be a little wet in wet weather by the side of the lake. Allow ¾ hour.

START From the car parking area just after you have driven past the end of the lake.

DIRECTIONS From Betws y Coed drive along the A5 towards Bangor. In Capel Curig turn left immediately before the Pinnacle Café on to the A4086 where there is a grassy triangle. Follow this road, passing Plas y Brenin the National Outdoor Centre, to the Pen y Gwryd. Continue straight ahead here and descend the twisting A498 to Llyn Gwynant. Continue past this and through Nantgwynant to reach Llyn Dinas on your left. Continue driving by the lake towards Beddgelert. Just beyond the end of the lake look out for a kissing gate and a finger post on your left. There is also a signed, long-stay parking area on your right. Park your car here.

Walk back up the road to the kissing gate by the finger post and go through. Follow the wide path to your right alongside the lake. In very wet weather this could be a short, shallow paddle. Continue to a footbridge. Cross over this above the wide fast flowing Afon Glaslyn and turn left at the far side to go through a kissing gate. Keep following the path by the lake and cross an often wide, fast flowing stream. There are many stones to stand on to keep dry as you cross. Continue to go over a ladder stile to reach a marker post beyond. Here the main path is indicated going to your right.

Instead of this turn left here and follow the very edge of the lake on a narrow path that leads to and over a ladder stile. Bear right to reach the junction with the main path at a marker post. Turn right here and walk over a footbridge. Continue up to, and climb over, a ladder stile. Pass by a ruin, over to your left, and continue easily up the gradually rising path. From the top of the rise rock steps lead down to an easy path that in turn leads down to the marker post of your outward walk. Retrace your steps from here back to your car.

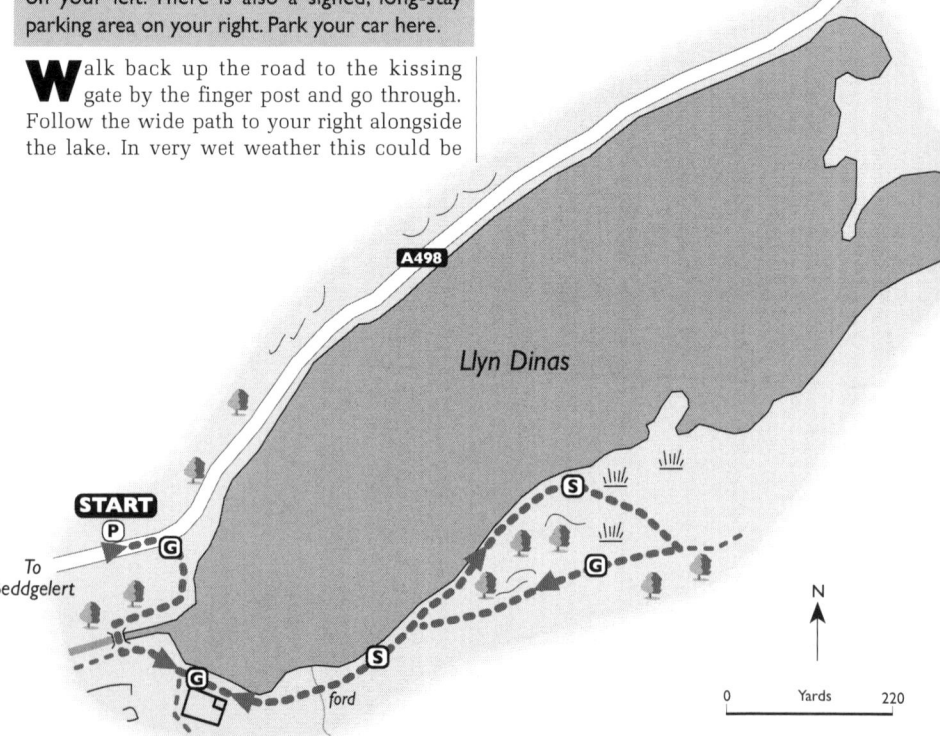

WALKS 7 & 8

WALK 8
AROUND LLYN CWMYSTRADLLYN

DESCRIPTION Although very boggy this 2¼ miles walk circumnavigating the perimeter of the lake is situated in a very quiet and pretty valley ringed with high mountains. Wellington boots are recommended. The paths are difficult to find in places and your route finding skills can be practised. Allow 1¾ hours.

START At the small car parking area beside the dam of Llyn Cwmystradllyn.

DIRECTIONS From Porthmadog follow the A487 towards Caernarfon. Drive through the small village of Penmorfa and continue to where signs indicate where you turn right towards Golan and Cwmystradllyn. Follow this road to a sign indicating a right turn into Cwmystradllyn. Follow this road, ignoring the turning to Prenteg, and pass the dramatic skeleton of an old slate mill up to your right and continue to the car parking area.

1 Go through the gate and walk across the dam. At the far side turn left on to a path that leads along the shore of the lake to a stile. Climb over this and continue to join an old wire fence. Follow the path alongside this and continue to a gate. Go through this and ignoring a stile to your left walk ahead keeping the dilapidated wire fence to your left. At a fence corner bear left. The path veers away from the fence to pass below a small rock bluff. Continue and cross a stream at the head of the lake just before a stile. Climb over this to reach some ruins.

2 Bear right here and then left to walk through tussocks to reach a fence. The fence descends into the lake. Climb over the stile and bear left on a faint path above the lake to reach the fence ahead. Keeping the fence to your right follow it until the path goes between a wall on the left and a fence on the right. Continue above a tiny wood on your left (in which there are some ruins). At a locked gate go down a rocky step and follow the path between the fence on your left and wall to your right. Go left over a stile in the fence by the end of a low rocky escarpment on your right. Turn right and follow the fence, keeping it on your right. When the fence ends at a wall climb over a stile on the right and then go through a gate immediately on your left. Follow the path along the water's edge and bear right below a gorse clad bluff and through a gap in the wall to a gate. Do NOT go through this but bear left keeping the fence to your right to a concrete footbridge. Cross over this and go through a gate immediately after, by a finger post. Turn right and walk up the field, keeping the wall to your right, to a gap (there is a redundant gate here). Go through this and follow the walled track, which is swampy at first, until two gates are reached. Go though the right hand one. In 100 yards you reach the narrow tarmac road. Turn left here and return to your car by the dam.

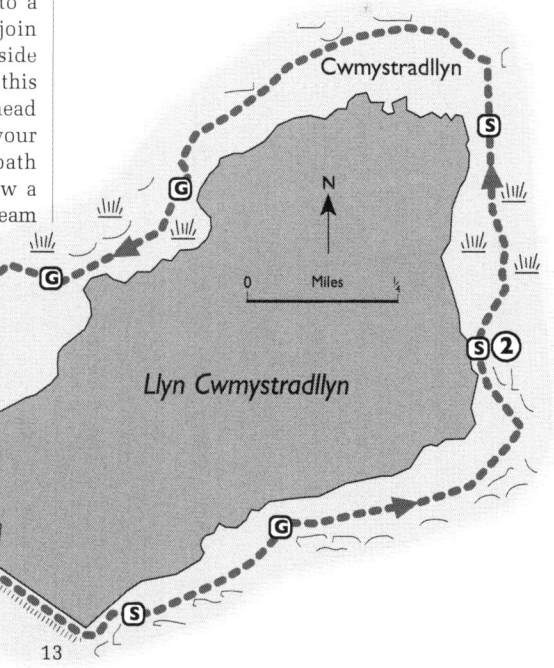

WALK 9
LLYN CWM Y FOEL, LLYNNAU DIFFWYS & LLYN CROESOR

DESCRIPTION This walk has some grand mountain scenery. Although it does not reach any summits it is a fine 6 mile walk with much of interest. Some route finding skills are necessary between Llyn Cwm y Foel, Llynnau Diffwys and until the good path leading down to Bwlch y Rhosydd is reached. There are scenes of much dereliction around the abandoned mines that were once thriving industries.

START From the Snowdonia National Park car park at Croesor.

DIRECTIONS From the Oakley Arms Hotel on the A487 near to Maentwrog turn right on to the B4410, signed to Rhyd. There is a turning to your left to Plas Tan y Bwlch, the Snowdonia National Park study centre, almost immediately after turning. Follow the B4410 passing Llyn Mair on your left to Garreg and turn right. Turn right again at the sign indicating Croesor in 2¼ miles ¼ mile a further. Follow the narrow road with care to the signed and obvious car park on your right.

1 Walk out of the car park over the footbridge and turn right. Go through ther kissing gate 10 yards further and continue along the path – an old tramway – noting the fine clapper bridge on your right. The path crosses an old tramway bridge to reach a gate. Go through this and continue to go through another gate to join a track. Walk straight ahead and climb over a ladder stile to the left of a gate and pass through the next gate 100 yards ahead. The track continues through a shallow cutting and up to another gate to the right of a fine slate fence.

2 Go through this gate and turn left down by the side of the slate fence keeping it on your left to a truncated wall on your right. Go over the footbridge at the end of the wall and head towards a ruin. Walk in front of this to reach a marker post and a more pronounced path. Follow this up as it crosses the hillside diagonally to reach a ladder stile. Climb over this. There are great views into Cwm Croesor from here. Keeping the fence to your left and then a wall continue up to where it veers left. Walk straight ahead here. The path now becomes vague but quickly reappears and continues past two large boulders. When the path runs out again by the remains of a wire fence go up and left to a post. Just beyond are the remains of some slate pillars. A series of small waterfalls are seen ahead. Walk above the slate pillars on a faint path to reach a stile in the fence. Go over this and follow the still faint path towards the waterfalls. The path improves to reach the top of the falls and after an easy scramble you reach the dam holding back the waters of Llyn Cwm y Foel.

3 Walk across the dam and bear right at the far side for 30 yards. There are now no paths! Go diagonally up and left towards a shallow grassy gully and walk up the right hand side of it, bearing slightly right to reach a path going right to left. Cross this and walk up another shallow gully on a faint path to the lower of the Llynnau Diffwys. A better path continues just below the lake to join another path going right to left. Cross straight over. Fifty yards further on join a very good path. Turn right and follow it down, but it is often very boggy, to reach a cairn by the side of a well marked track. Turn left along this heading towards the ruins of Rhosydd Slate Mine. Climb over a ladder stile to view the desolation of a once thriving industry.

14

WALK 9

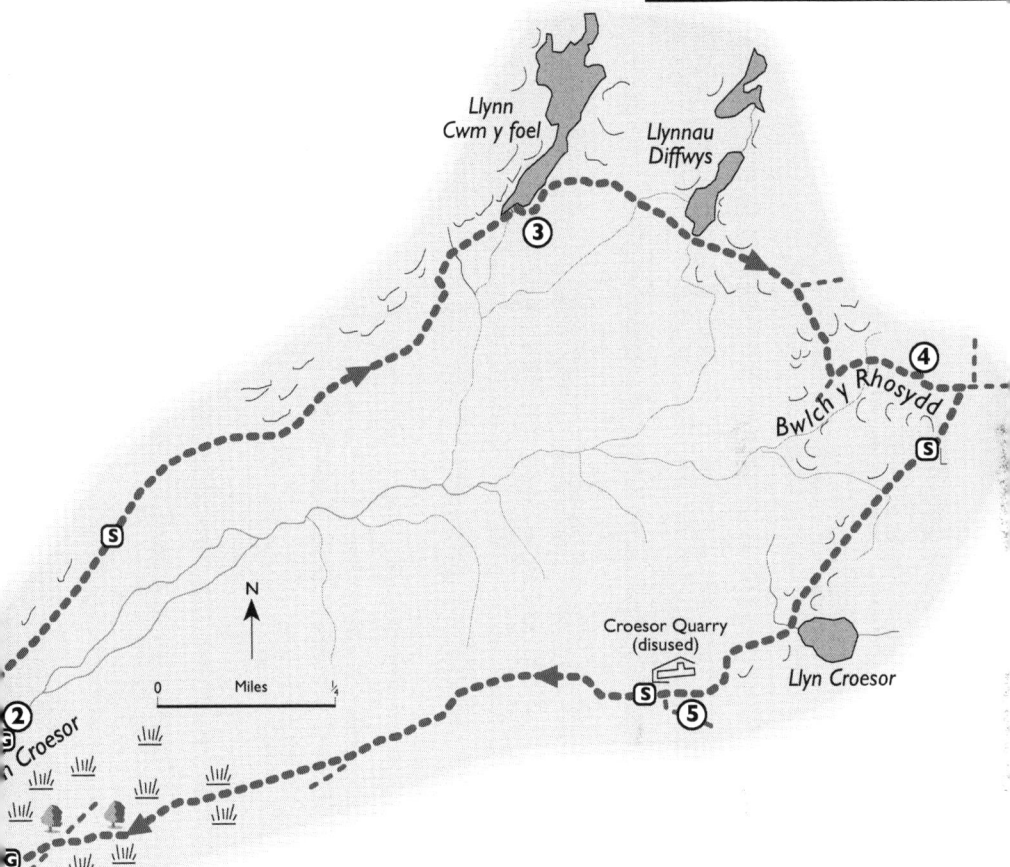

4 Bear right before entering the ruins and right again by the gable end of the ruined house. This is to the right of a deeply incised gully above which is a huge spoil heap. A faint path appears then disappears in swampy ground as a ladder stile is approached. Climb over this. Bear right on a faint path to avoid the bog and then go left to join the obvious path ahead. Follow this to the partially drained Llyn Croesor. Go through the top of the dam on the walled path. A more gradual ascent now continues to where it descends to the desolate Croesor Slate Mine.

5 Walk through the ruins and climb over a ladder stile on the left. Follow the good track down and through a gate above the first farm. The track continues down through another gate to reach a four way junction. Walks half right past the houses on your right to a track junction. Go through the gate of your outward walk – on your left – and continue back to your car in the car park

WALK 10
LLYN NEWYDD, LLYN BOWYDD & LLYN DRUM-BOETH

DESCRIPTION This is an interesting 4 mile walk that also has some tremendous views. There are close up views of three other lakes, Llyn Du-bach, Llyn Glas and the furthest one, Llyn y Manod. There are two very short pathless sections that are easily dealt with. Once away from the quarry workings there is a sense of remoteness.

START At the car park, close to the 'Slate World' shop.

DIRECTIONS From the north or the south follow the A470 into Blaenau Ffestiniog. Opposite the turning down to the station turn left, if coming from the north, or right if coming from the south to park in the large car park by the side of 'Slate World' where there are toilets. There is a small fee payable.

1 From the car park walk to the main road and turn left along the high street to Lord Street. This is opposite Cwmbowydd Road on your right. Turn left up Lord Street. The road becomes steep beyond the last cottages on your left. The tarmac ends at a kissing gate. Go through the gate and follow the track through spoil heaps on each side. There is a four way junction just after the track levels out. Turn left to meet another track and turn left along it with increasingly good views of Llyn Trawsfynydd and the Rhinog Mountains as height is gained. Keep following the track to a cattle grid.

2 Turn right 25 yards before this up a stony, disused track to the right of a stream. This track meets another. Turn right along this and follow it up past a fenced pond on your right to reach a 'Y' junction. Take the left arm of the 'Y' and walk past another pond, this one to your left. The track continues and passes through two gates in quick succession to where there is a fence on your right. You will note a way marker on the last fence post. Turn right here and follow a vague path in the direction indicated to cross a tiny clapper bridge. Climb over the stile by a pole just beyond and walk up to the obvious pipe ahead. Follow this up to where there is a concrete leat. This continues to your right and is follwed for 30 yards to an open pipe. Take the narrow path just above the pipe and rejoin it until it goes underground. A vague path continues ahead past some uncovered sections to the top of an incline with the remains of the winding house to your right.

3 Turn left along the track and go through a gate. The track continues to where the dam holding back the water of Llyn Newydd is seen to your left. This is just before two upended concrete pipes. Leave the track and walk up to the lake. Return to the track and turn left. Walk down into a dip and back up again. Continue to where Llyn Bowydd suddenly appears. Walk along the top of the dam until it ends. Turn sharp right and down a vague path. The path becomes lost so continue around a rocky knoll and then bear left to a substantial wall on your left. Follow this by going slightly up and then down to a waymarked ladder stile. Climb over this to reach a path. This veers away from the wall and continues to a dilapidated stile just before Llyn Drum-boeth.

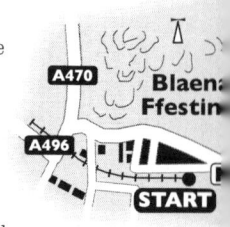

4 It is safer to cross the fallen wall. Bear left on a much more defined path through small spoil heaps with increasingly glorious views. The path continues along the level top of a spoil heap to where a steep descent leads down – CARE as slate is sharp and can cause nasty cuts – and continues to another winding house, where here is a waymark. Walk down the incline to a stone hut on your right. Turn left here down some steps. Follow the good path bearing right. Pass to the right of a grassy/rock knoll and walk down a system of inclines heading

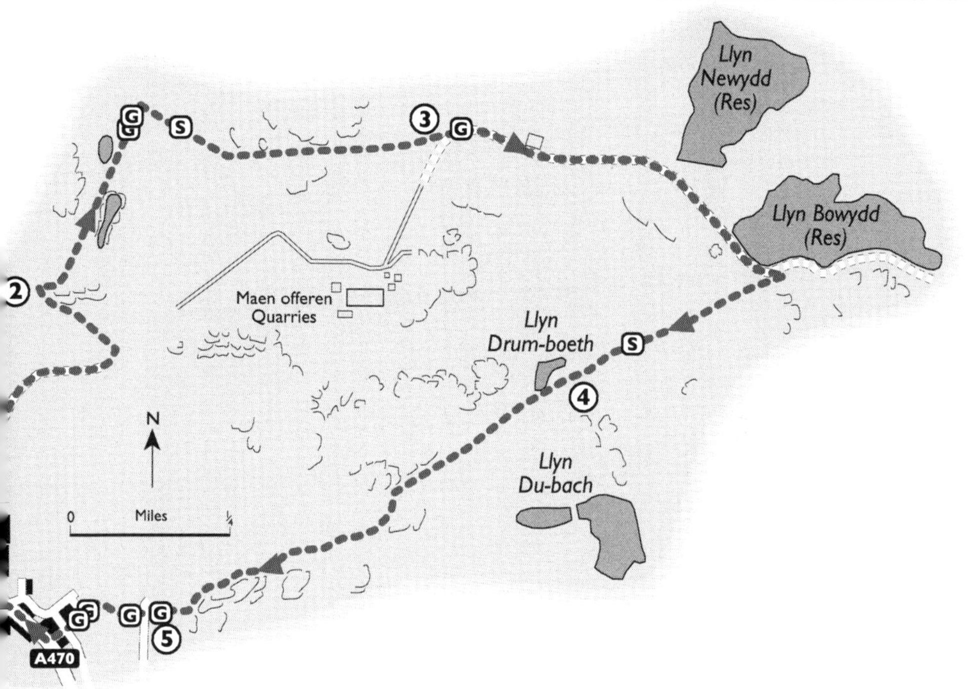

WALK 10

towards the right edge of a conifer plantation ahead. When you reach the track above it turn right and follow it down to a gate.

5 Go through this and a small ornate one on your right 15 yards further. Follow the path down to a fence and continue down to where the path veers right to a gate to the left of a house. Go though this and another 20 yards further to reach a road. Walk straight ahead down the steep road – there is a helpful railing to your right – to join the A470. Turn right along this back to your car.

Llyn Bowydd

WALK 11
LLYN ARENIG FAWR

DESCRIPTION This is a grand 3¼ mile (3½ miles if taking the longer option) walk visiting a dramatic and remote mountain lake in the Arenigs. Unfortunately there are no satisfactory walks around Llyn Celyn but you return close to, but above it giving good views of the western end. Allow 2 hours for the slightly shorter walk and 2½ hours for the longer.

START From a lay-by off the narrow road at the start of the track.

DIRECTIONS From the A470 turn onto the A4212 near Trawsfynydd and drive towards Bala. Follow this road for 8 miles to where there is a left turn onto the B4391 towards Ffestiniog. Almost opposite this turning and to the right is a sign for Arenig. Turn right onto this minor road and follow it for 2 miles to where there are several small parking areas off the road on your left near a track leading off up the hill to your right.

1 From your car go to the start of the track and immediately climb over a stile. Follow the track up, steeply at first and then more gradually to where it levels out and where Llyn Arenig Fawr is seen ahead. Keep walking along the track to reach the dam. Bear left to a stone hut. This is a bothy belonging to the Mountain Bothies Association. Please respect this.

2 Continue down keeping the wall and fence to your right. The path becomes narrow and goes through heather to reach a ladder stile just before a stream. Climb over the stile and turn right to the footbridge. Cross this and bear left back to the path (in low water the stream may be crossed directly via a stepping stone). Follow it up through a short boggy section to reach a faint path going from right to left. Turn left and follow it to a prominent wall corner. Follow the wall on your left to reach a finger post at the junction with the road. Turn left along it back to your car.

3 OR ALTERNATIVELY if you want a closer view of the lake – cross over the road to the marker post. Follow a vague track to a wall and follow this down to a stile where the wall turns right. Climb over the stile and bear left to a broken wall. Follow this down and go through two gates to join the dismantled railway. Turn left along this and bear left up the access road to the minor road. Turn right along this back to your car.

The 117 feet deep Llyn Arenig was adapted as a reservoir in 1830 and supplies Bala. The pipeline was laid in 1879. In certain conditions strange echoes resembling a piano being played can be heard. The 'Tylwith Teg' or fairies have strong links here. Like other lakes there is a legend relating to a young shepherd discovering a bull calf in the rushes. He took it home and looked after it. The calf grew into a fine bull and sired many fine offspring. Years later the shepherd was once again walking around the lake when he saw a small man with a flute singing and calling his cattle back to the water. The cattle had names – Mulican, Molican, Malens and Mair.

Llyn Arenig Fawr

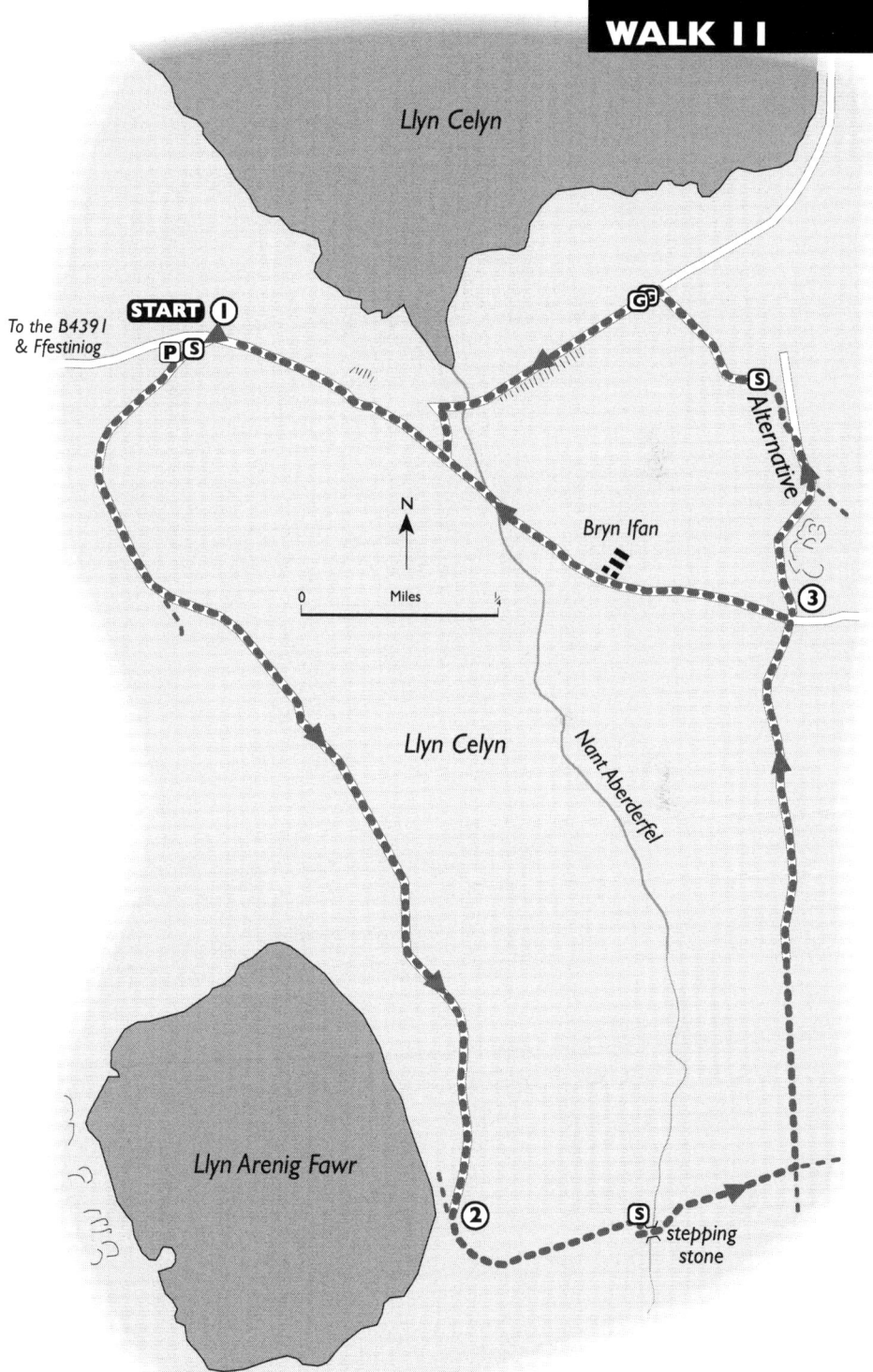

WALK 12
LLYN YR OERFEL & LLYN CRAIG-Y-TAN

DESCRIPTION This is an extremely scenic 3½ miles walk having superb views of Llyn Trawsfynydd most of the way. There are also exceptional views of the Moelwyns, Rhinogau and Llŷn. Although there are paths and tracks there are gaps and these will test your route finding abilities in a not too serious situation. Allow 1¾ hours.

START At the Snowdonia National Park car park for Tomen-y-Mur.

DIRECTIONS From Blaenau Ffestiniog follow the A470 towards Dolgellau. At the junction with the A487 turn left and after a ¼ mile turn left again onto a minor road and follow this under the old railway bridge to the car parking area on your right. OR, from Dolgellau, follow the A470 towards Betws y Coed and turn right ¼ mile before the A487 junction and where the A470 turns right. Follow the minor road under the old railway bridge as above.

1 From your car walk up the road to a junction with a track – finger post way marker. Follow the track as it rises easily to where it levels and continues past the turning for the very isolated house – *Tir-y-Mynydd* – by Llyn yr Oerfel. Continue along the track a further 300 yards looking carefully for a faint path which branches left. This is some 100 yards before the ruins seen to your right.

2 The path becomes more distinct and parallels the track 50 yards to your right as it rises above an old quarry – Braich-ddu. The path joins a grassy track. Follow this gradually up with increasingly fine views of the Rhinogau and Llyn Trawsfynydd. Avoid a swampy area to the left to where it can be crossed easily and dry where an obvious grassy path rises up at the far side of the bog to the left of a rocky bluff. There is a small lake down to your right here. Climb up the path to the top of the bluff and bear diagonally right along an obvious slope, where there is no path! – *but a superb view of Llyn Trawsfynydd.* Keep following the rake to where a faint track appears. The track bends left – this is almost opposite the far end of the small lake – to reach a VERY boggy area, thankfully short. Keep to the left of it for a drier crossing and around the toe of a small rocky ridge. There is a weed filled lake to your right. Once around the toe of the bluff keep to the dry high ground above the next boggy area heading towards a wall and a well marked path to the left of it seen ahead. *Another dam of interesting construction appears unexpectedly holding back the water of another weed filled lake.* A small stream flows from beneath the dam.

3 Cross the stream easily and bear up and right to a much better defined path. Follow this up to the top of a grassy knoll overlooking the very pretty Llyn Craig-y-Tan. *There are exceptional and breath taking views from here. It is difficult to tear oneself away.* Continuing down to the shore. At first head towards the conifer forest but bearing left on an obvious path along a broad grassy ridge that parallels the forest 300 yards to the left of it. The path becomes a track and veers left to pass by a ruined, ancient, walled

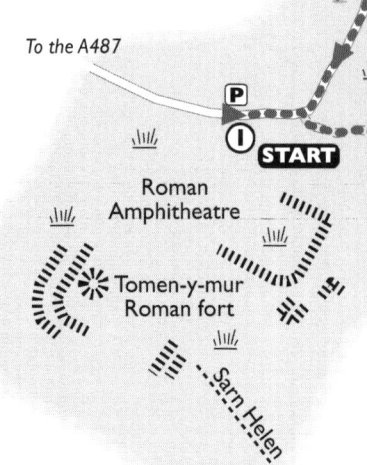

To the A487

Roman Amphitheatre

Tomen-y-mur Roman fort

Sarn Helen

START

WALK 12

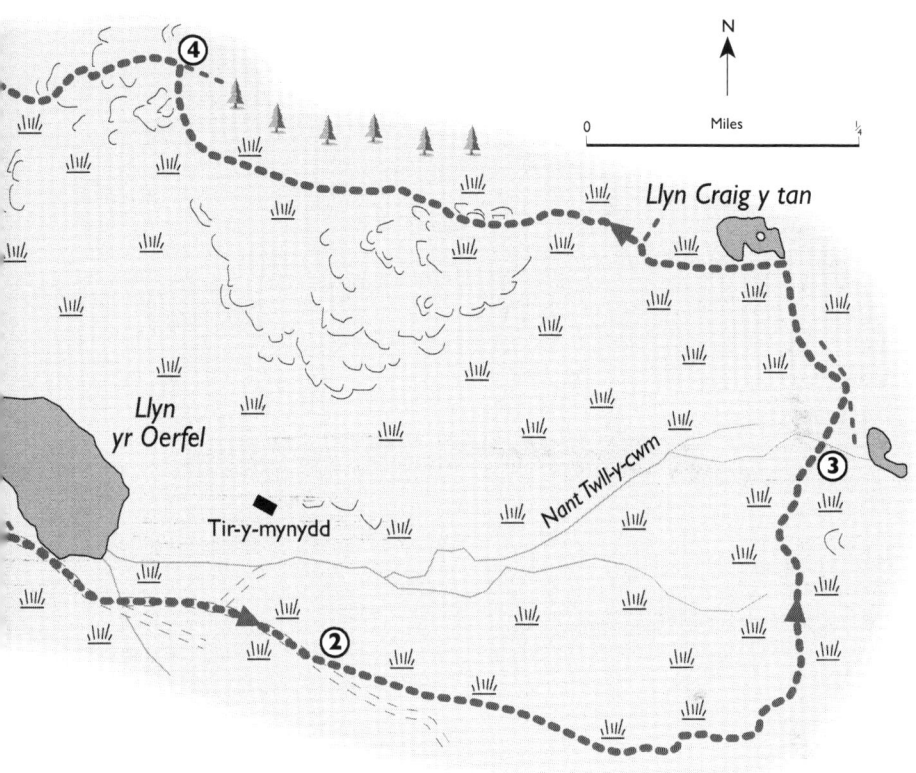

enclosure seen to your right. Keep walking down and where the track appears to end almost opposite the end of the forest a narrow faint path goes right towards it. Pass below the forest and cross a tiny stream.

4 Follow the path that becomes a track. Bear left towards the stream with another small walled enclosure above it. The track is now very distinct and is followed to where an obvious but faint path descends parallel to the stream 50 yards to your left to join another very obvious track. Go left down this to the tarmac road. Turn left along this back to your car.

It is worth visiting Tomen-y-Mur and the Roman Fort. The fort was built in 78 AD. after Agricola's campaign and was possibly named Branogenium or Mediomanium. The actual mound of Tomen-y-Mur was built much later and is the remnant of a Norman motte and bailey fortification. It is known to have been associated with William Rufus in 1095.

WALK 13
LLYN MAIR & COED HAFOD Y LLYN

DESCRIPTION This is a lovely 2½ mile walk visiting two very pretty lakes. At a short section of cleared forest there are great views of the Moelwyns. If you time your walk to be at one of the railway crossings you will be met by the cheery waves from the driver and passengers enjoying the Ffestiniog Railway journey. Most of the walking is on forest tracks but with sections of paths that are easy to follow. Allow 1½ hours.

START At the car park belonging to the Countryside Council for Wales by the side of Llyn Mair.

DIRECTIONS From Porthmadog follow the A487 towards Maentwrog and Dolgellau. At the Oakeley Arms Hotel turn left on to the B4410 towards Rhyd. Continue for ¾ mile to the small car park on your right across from Llyn Mair.

1 Leave the car park and carefully cross the road to the double gate. Go through this to reach a fine picnic site as well as entering the National Nature Reserve. Bear right past the tables along a track to a gap by the side of a gate. Beyond the gap follow the track to a junction where you will spot marker post 26. Go left here and follow the wide path through a gap in the wall to enter Coed Hafod y Llyn. Keep on the path and cross a footbridge for the stream outlet from the fine pond above you. Follow the path by the lake to a seat on your left. The path continues around the shore of the lake to point 10 where a track goes up to your right on concrete strips. Ignore this and continue alongside the lake, through a gap in a wall and up to another seat. Continue another 50 yards to point 11.

2 Turn acutely to your right and walk away from the lake. Continue up the track past a huge multi limbed beech tree. 50 yards beyond this turn up to your right by a beech tree with twin trunks. Turn right up 4 steps and ascend the path to the Ffestiniog Railway. Climb over the stile and cross the line carefully looking out for trains. Walk up steps and through a gate. Bear right. Walk up to a house on your left and continue to a track junction. Go left and follow it to another track junction. Straight ahead leads up to Hafod y Llyn. Turn left and continue past point 5 to point 6. Bear right through the cleared area on your right – where there are great views of the Moelwyns – to point 7. Go left here to point 31 and continue along the track ignoring a turning right down to a white gate. At point 30 where there is a finger post on your right keep following the track bearing left above the pretty Llyn Hafod y Llyn. Continue past a junction on your left to another finger post. This one is to your left. Keep on the track and walk down to point 16. Continue to a seat seen up to your right.

3 Turn right 20 yards beyond this down a good path and pass a picnic table. Continue following the gentle path as it meanders lazily to the dam. Cross this and walk up to the finger post at point 30. Turn left along the track, then left again 50 yards further on and descend to the white gate seen previously. Looking out for trains carefully cross the line and over the stile at the far side. Walk down the track passing point 28 and continuing to point 27. At the track junction here go to your left and walk along to a gate. This bypassed by walking to the right of it. Continue down the track to point 26 and familiar ground. Go straight ahead back to your car in the car park.

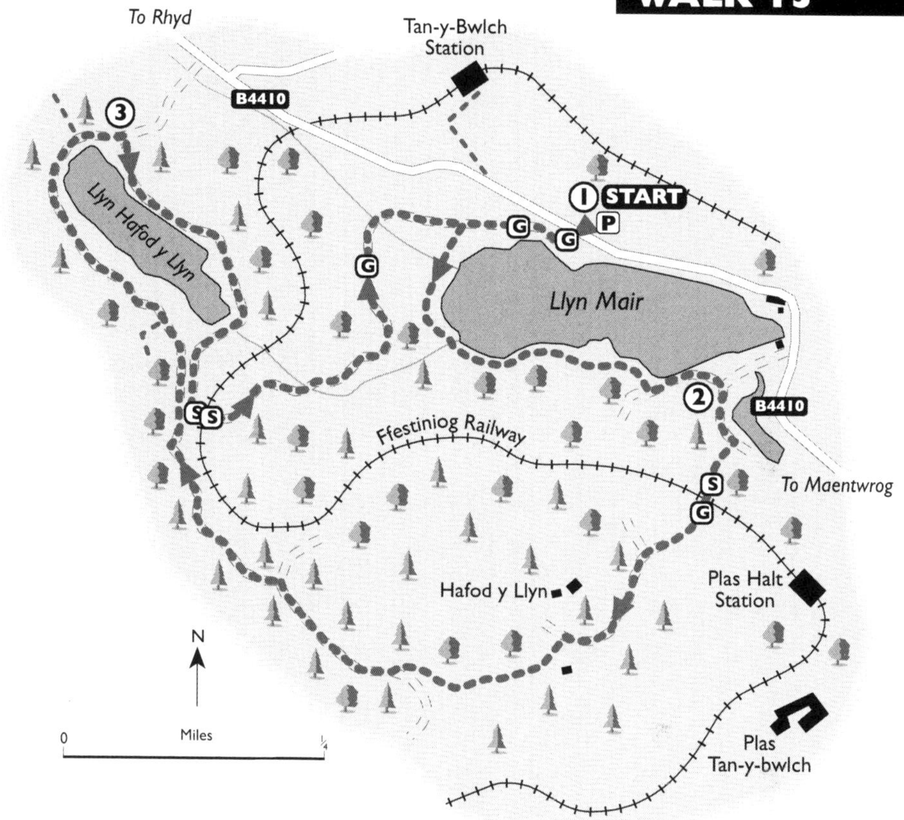

WALK 13

These woodlands are very special and are of European importance. They are designated a Special Area for Conservation (SAC) because of the large extent of oak woodland with the damp habitat providing ideal conditions for mosses, ferns, liverworts and lichens. Hundreds of species can be found in the area. The rare Lesser Horseshoe Bat has its European stronghold here.

Llyn Mair was built in 1889 with Llyn Hafod y Llyn being formed around the same time. Just past point 2 is the millpond, seen down to your left. Water from here supplied power for electricity generation for Plas Tan y Bwlch and the village of Maentwrog as well as supplying power for the saw and flour mills.

Llyn Mair

WALK 14
LLYN TECWYN ISAF & LLYN TECWYN UCHAF

DESCRIPTION This is a very pleasant 2½ mile walk through some fine woodland visiting two very pretty lakes. There are spectacular views of the Dwyryd Estuary from the church. The short sections of road are very quiet. Allow 1½ hours.

START At a small lay-by by the side of the lake.

DIRECTIONS From Harlech follow the A496 towards Porthmadog. Turn right off this road in Talsarnau just beyond the Ship Aground pub seen on your left where the road is signed for Llandecwyn 1¼ miles. Follow the narrow minor road to a left turn where Llandecwyn is again signed. Follow this to the tiny hamlet and bear left at the 'T' junction, where there is a telephone box on your right, and follow this dead end road to the lake where there is a small lay-by on your right by the lake just before a 'Y' junction.

1 With your back to the lake walk to your right. At the 'Y' junction bear right and continue alongside the lake. Turn up to your left 200 yards from the 'Y' junction at a finger post indicating a Llwybr Chyoeddus. Walk up the wide path and go through a long redundant gate where the path levels. Keeping the fence to your right walk around a boggy area to where the path veers left and slightly up to pass through gorse bushes. Go through a gap in the fence to enter a lovely sessile oak wood – *and scented heather in late August*. At a path junction bear right and down to pass over a low stone wall down some stone steps. A well marked path continues slightly up and then descends gradually to a gate. Go through this and join a narrow tarmac road by a waymark. Walk up the road for a ½ mile to where it levels. *There is a picturesque house to your left.*

2 Turn to your left by the side of the house and go through a gate 20 yards from the road. There is a waymark here. Enter a garden. Please respect the privacy of the residents. Bear right as indicated. At the top of the garden go through a kissing gate and follow the path alongside the wall on your right. Where the wall turns right keep straight ahead and continue to a wall. Keeping the wall to your left follow it up to where there is a sudden view of Llyn Tecwyn Uchaf. Go through a gap in the wall. There is a waymark and ladder stile to the right almost at the lake shore. Follow the path through a boggy area alongside the wall on your left to a ladder stile over the wall. Climb over this and follow the path close to the lake. After a short easy rock step descend to a fine shingle beach. Just before the dam another easy rock step leads to where it is easy to walk across the dam to a gate.

3 Go through the gate and join a track. Turn left along it to another gate above a smaller dam. Go through this and bear left at a track junction 20 yards beyond. Ignore the way marker on your right. Continue up the track alongside the wall on your right. Keep following the track and descend to go through a gate. Continue down to the church and superb views of the Dwyryd Estuary. Continue down the road to your car by the side of Llyn Tecwyn Isaf.

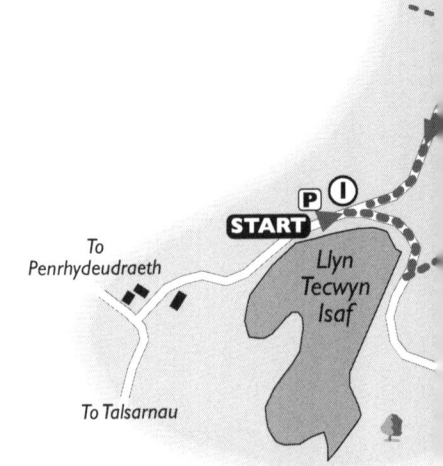

WALK 14

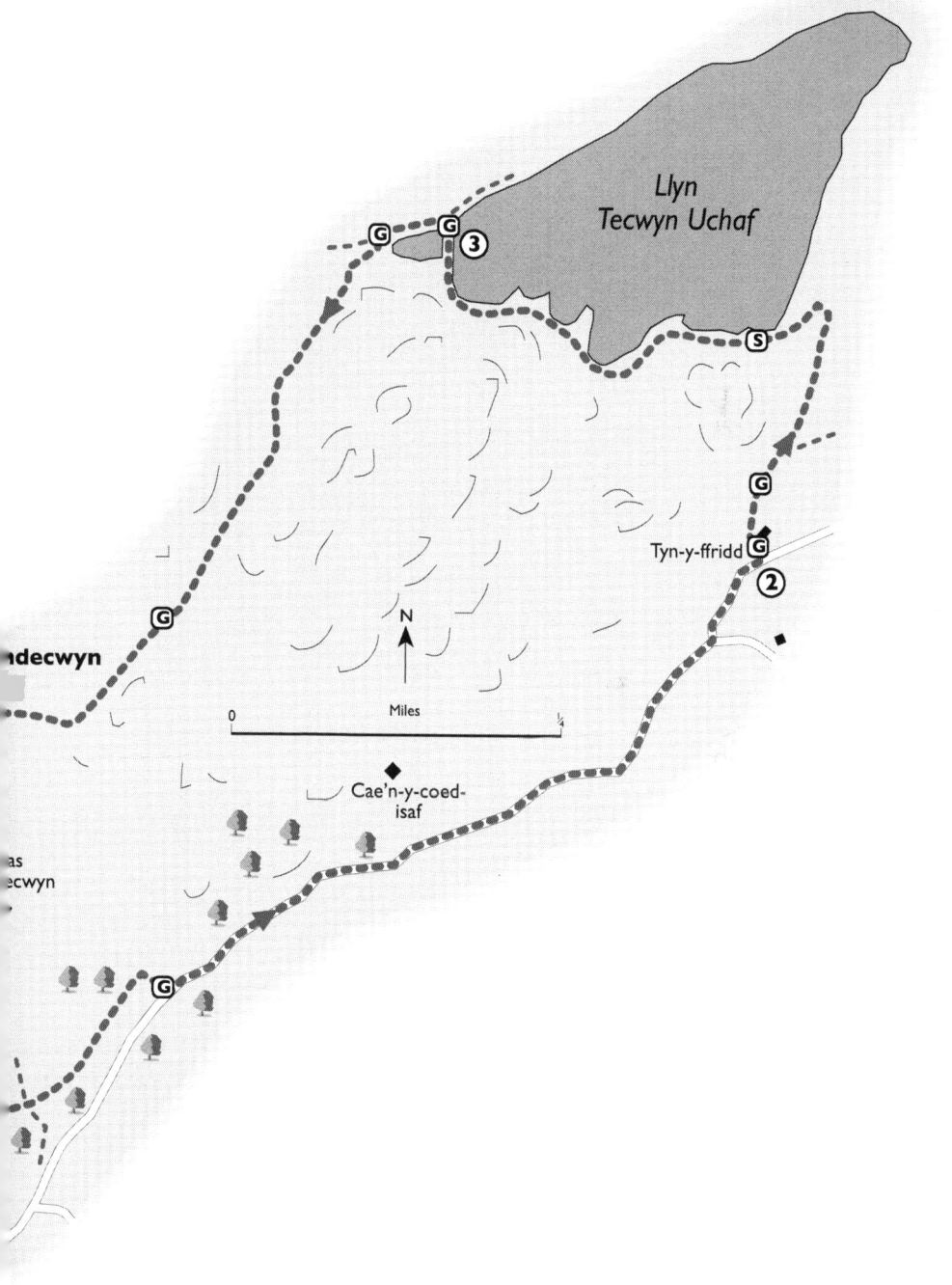

WALK 15
LLYN Y PARC

DESCRIPTION This is a lovely 4¼ mile walk through woodland to a tranquil lake. It makes an excellent companion walk to Llyn Elsi (see Volume 1) – one in the morning and the other in the afternoon! There are the remains of the Aberllyn lead and zinc mine, a fine, though small waterfall and a tumbling stream. Allow 2 hours.
START From the Pont y Pair car park in Betws y Coed.
DIRECTIONS From the A5 in Betws y Coed turn onto the B5106 that leads to Trefriw. Turn left immediately after crossing the bridge and then right into the car park, small fee payable. There are toilets here.

1 Walk out of the car park, turn right, and walk up the road. Turn right at the first turning on your right. Continue along this road to where there is a path indicator board. Your walk follows the yellow route, although at times the posts are spread well apart. Turn right to walk around the barrier on its left and continue gradually up the track to the top of the rise. Just after this on your left is a marker post. Turn left here. Follow the path to a four-way junction. Continue straight ahead, where there is a marker post, to enter the very steep sided Aberllyn Ravine. Follow the path up this with a lovely tumbling stream to your right. The path becomes steep and rocky at this point. Partway up there is a well marked path on your right going slightly down which leads to a gated entrance leading into the Aberllyn lead and zinc mine. Continue up past further two securely gated entrances on your left. The second one is very close to a pretty but small waterfall on your right.

2 Continue alongside the stream and cross the footbridge to reach a track. Follow this passing a gate on your left leading to Aberllyn Cottage. At the track junction turn right, although a rest and a sit down on the seat overlooking Llyn y Parc is recommended before continuing. Continue along the track until you reach a wooden marker post.

Turn left here and pass the coloured marker post immediately beyond. Bear right and follow the delightful path alongside the lake. At the end of the lake the path climbs up to a track. Turn right along it and continue to reach a four-way junction. Turn right and continue back to the seat at the track junction. Retrace you outward walk back to your car.

*L*lyn y Parc *is a natural lake although it contains no fish due to the high lead content. The dam was built to raise the water level to provide water to power the machinery at the mine. In 1900 two hundred men were employed. There are six levels and the most productive period was between 1850 and 1919.*

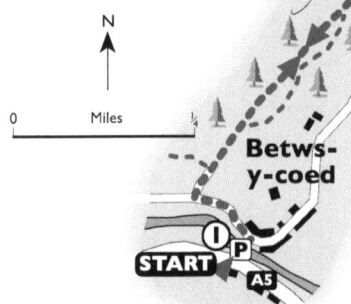

WALKS 15 & 16

WALK 16
LLYN TAN-Y-GRAIG

DESCRIPTION This one mile walk is ideal for an evening stroll when the sun highlights the huge ramparts of Cadair Idris. The lake is a hidden gem and is a joy at any time. Allow an hour.

START At the western end of the lay-by 330 yards from the roundabout in Llanelltyd, along the Barmouth road.

DIRECTIONS From Dolgellau follow the A470 towards Betws y Coed. At the roundabout in Llanelltyd turn left on to the A496 towards Barmouth. Turn right at some railings and along this road to park at its end. There is a footpath sign indicating the start of the New Precipice Walk and a surfaced access road between two houses.

Follow the tarmac path beside Tyn-yr-ardd uphill until it ends and continue up the stony track to a metal kissing gate. Go through and follow the path with a fence to your right. This is quite steep at first but becomes less so to reach a post on your left at a level area. An obvious path bears left up the hillside to reach a ladder stile. Climb over this and walk ahead 50 yards to reach a grassy track. Follow this up and continue to the lake. Turn left. Climb over the stile, bearing right on the path to walk over a short embankment. Turn right just beyond on a less clear path to reach a better defined one that follows the far side of the lake. At the end of the lake the path reaches a pronounced ditch with a small bridge spanning it. Bear right, go through a metal gate and cross the small dam to reach a metal post indicating that swimming is not allowed. An undulating path continues above the lake to the top of a grassy knoll where there are great views of Cadair Idris and the surrounding area. Descend to meet the track of your outward walk. Turn left down it and back to Llanelltyd.

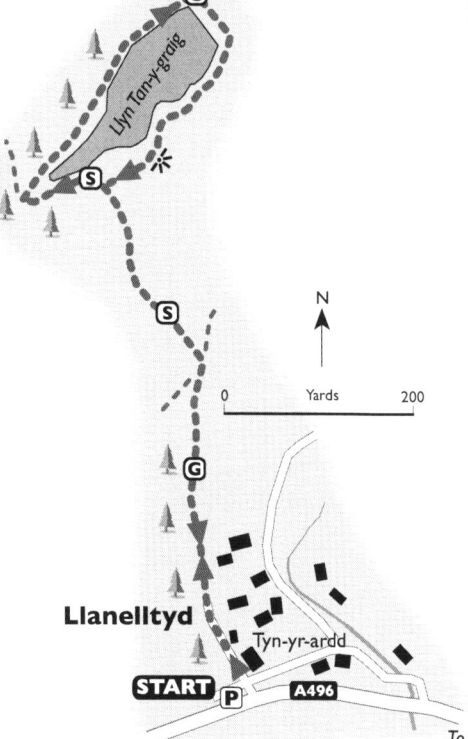

Llyn Tan-y-graig

WALK 17
LLYN TRAWSFYNYDD

DESCRIPTION This is a very fine 8 mileswalk with a short section along the main A470, fortunately on a wide footpath. Views are, in places, spectacular. The long footbridge spanning the lake is unique, not to be missed! There are short sections of uphill but are easily climbed. Allow 4½ hours.

START At the café and fishing permit office car park just off the A470 down the road to the power station.

DIRECTIONS From the south follow the A470 from Dolgellau towards Betws y Coed to the obvious turn left down the access road to the Llyn Trawsfynydd Magnox Power Station. Follow this road for 100 yards and turn left. Park your car in the café parking area. From the north follow the A470 towards Dolgellau but turn right into the access road and park as above.

1 Leave the car park by the information board and follow the track around a gate passing to the left of the fishermen's car parking area across to your right. Walk straight ahead where there is a sign indicating the direction to the Bailey bridge. Bear left and cross a footbridge to follow the path passing several information panels and cross another footbridge. The path continues and passes a picnic table to your right with the following inscription – *Pandy Ddwyryd's fold and scythe be idle, While fish and fowl cruise the lake.* Go through a gate to join a very narrow row road. Turn right along it and continue to a fine picnic area and a 'Y' junction of path and track. Bear left passing through a gate and follow the path by the lake. Cross a footbridge and follow the path on the right of a stream up to twin metal posts. Bear left and pass through two metal gates to reach the A470.

2 Turn right along this and right again ¾ mile further into the village of Trawsfynydd. Continue through the village – where there are shops, pubs and toilets – to the Cross Foxes pub. Turn right opposite this down Cefn Gwyn. Turn right again at the 'T' junction and pass through a gate by a finger post. Follow the track to where a finger post indicates where you turn left off the track following a path across a field. Go through a gate at the far side and continue through a gateless gap and down through another gate just before the ¼ mile long footbridge across the dam lake. Walk across this remarkable feature.

3 At the far end go down steps and follow the edge of the dam crossing a stile. Continue to a ladder stile on your right. DO NOT cross this but go down to your left and through a kissing gate to reach a narrow tarmac road. Follow this to your right and continue to a 'Y' junction. Bear right here and follow the road passing the headquarters for the South Snowdon Search and Rescue Team. Just past the no through road sign go through a gate. At the top of a small rise is a passing place and finger post. Ignore this and continue along the road. Just beyond the cattle grid sign there is a 'Y' junction.

4 Turn left following the indicated footpath – NOT the road – signed to the Main Dam and Maentwrog. Follow the walled path up to and over a waymarked ladder stile. Continue past another waymark on an oak tree on the left of the path and climb over another ladder stile. Continue with the wall on your right and climb yet another ladder stile. Ford the small stream and go through a gate. Walk up the rough track and the grassier continuation with the wall still to your right. Cross the next ladder stile to reach a sign indicating the way to the Dam on your left. Walk up by a line of poles to reach a wider path. Go right and up. Just after the path levels go over a stile and walk straight ahead to a post 100 yards ahead. Continue down the narrow grassy path – *the dam is seen ahead here, along with great views of the Moelwyns.* The path becomes rougher as it descends to meet the wall bounding the wood on your right.

WALK 17

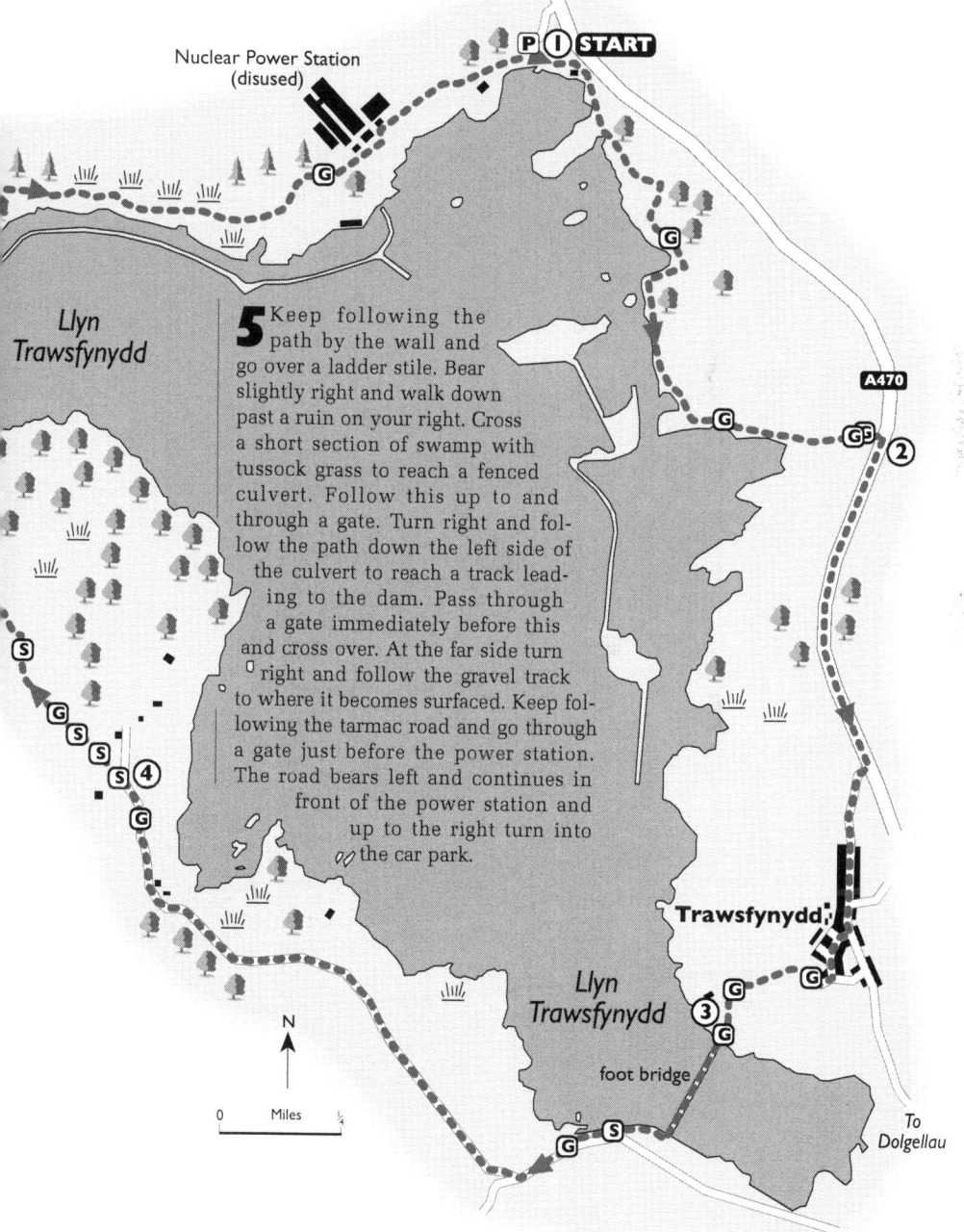

5 Keep following the path by the wall and go over a ladder stile. Bear slightly right and walk down past a ruin on your right. Cross a short section of swamp with tussock grass to reach a fenced culvert. Follow this up to and through a gate. Turn right and follow the path down the left side of the culvert to reach a track leading to the dam. Pass through a gate immediately before this and cross over. At the far side turn right and follow the gravel track to where it becomes surfaced. Keep following the tarmac road and go through a gate just before the power station. The road bears left and continues in front of the power station and up to the right turn into the car park.

WALK 18
LLYN CLYWEDOG

DESCRIPTION This 2½ mile walk is surprisingly little travelled even though there is an informative leaflet available. It is a very scenic and lovely walk with continuous superb views over this large tract of water and surrounding countryside. Allow 1½ hours for the walk but longer if you decide to have a picnic at one of the numerous sites.

START At a small pull in just beyond the roadside Nature Trail sign on the minor road that goes around the lake.

DIRECTIONS From Llanidloes take the Mountain Road towards Forge signed for Staylittle and Machynlleth. Turn left at the signs for the Bryn-Tail Lead Mine and continue down this minor road passing by the right turn to the mine. Continue on the road to a prominent Severn Trent sign indicating a right turn to Llyn Clywedog and snack bar. Keep on the road – unless you fancy a coffee break – and drive up to a grassy area by a cattle grid. This is the alternative starting point. Drive over the brow of the hill and descend to a picnic area on the right of the road close to the Nature Trail sign. There is parking on your right 30 yards beyond the tables.

1 From your car walk back to the Nature Trail sign and turn left through a gate. Continue past the house to a stile to the left of a gate. Cross this to enter a field. Walk down this keeping close to the fence on your left past a prominent marker post bearing left as indicated to reach a gate – stop 1. Go through this and follow the path down between fences to another gate not far from the lake. Go through this and descend steps to a finger post – stop 2. Turn right. (Left is for Glyndwr's Way). The well marked path continues just above the lake to stop 5 and a gate. Go through this and turn left. (Going right here is for the much shorter walk of a mile). Walk over a footbridge and through another gate. Keep following the path just above the lake shore passing two information boards to a large white pole at the end of the peninsula.

2 Turn right and walk upslope to a substantial fence on your left and follow this quite steeply aided by steps in parts to a bench at stop 12. There are good views of the lake from here. Continue up the fine ridge with increasingly expansive views of the lake on both sides to a picnic table close to the summit. This is a grand place to have a picnic. The view down to the dam is quite remarkable as there appears to be just a flimsy wall holding all that water back and the lake looks like it is suspended above a huge void below! Bear right to stop 13 and still bearing to your right reach a small stand of larch trees. Descend from here bearing left past another picnic table to a kissing gate. Go through this and follow the fence on your left over a grassy knoll to go through another kissing gate at a fence junction. Keep following the fence then wall on your left to the final kissing gate. Go through to join the tarmac road and turn right along it for the short walk back to your car.

Llyn Clywedog was built between 1964 and 1967. It is the tallest mass concrete dam in Britain at 236 feet high and almost 755 feet long. It holds back a staggering 11,000 million gallons of water and is 216 feet deep at its maximum depth. In total it stretches for 6 miles covering an area of 615 acres. To appreciate the dam fully it is recommended that after this walk, and to make more of your day, you walk the Clywedog Gorge and Bryn-Tail Mine trail. Although taking 30 minutes or so it also gives you the experience of looking around an old lead mine. There is a leaflet for this available from the snack bar.

WALK 18

Clywedog Dam

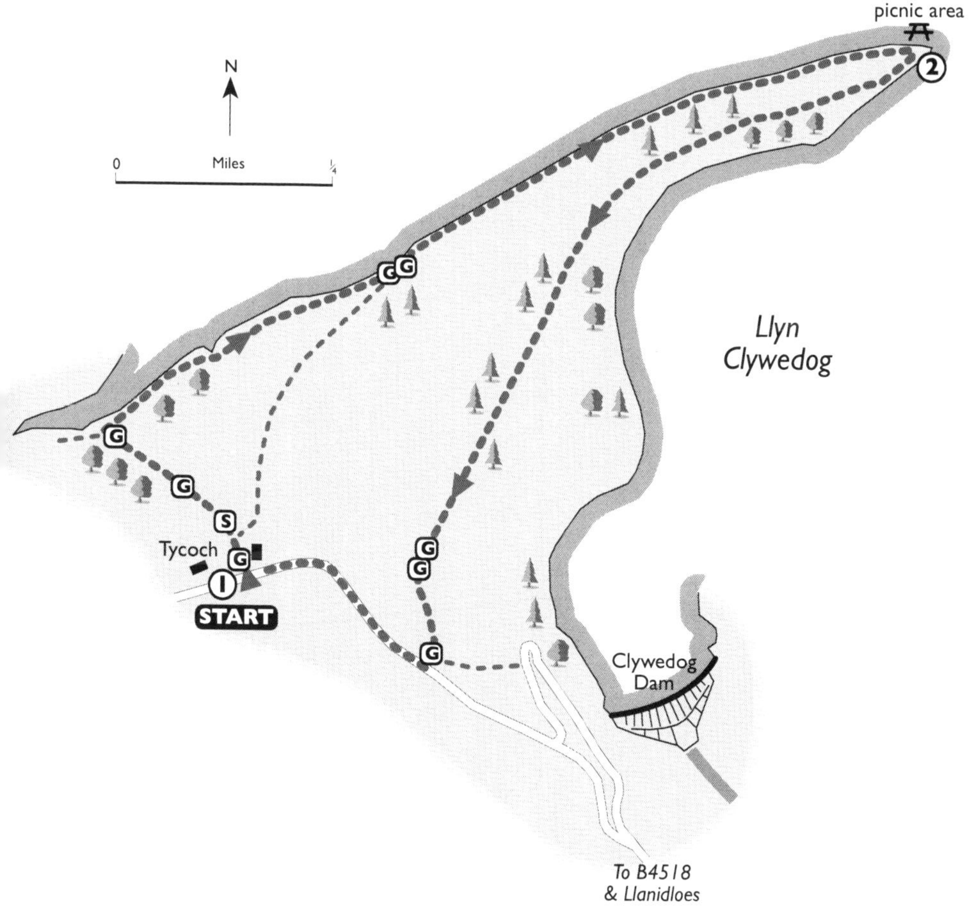

WALK 19
LLYN TRWYR COED & POND LLYWERNOG FROM NANT YR ARIAN

DESCRIPTION These are pretty stretches of water enhanced by many Red Kites, especially at feeding times. (15.00 in the summer and 14.00 in winter). There are information 'signals' along the trail that follows a smooth gravel path through woodland which is well signed with marker posts. The walk is accessible to all. Allow 45 minutes for the stroll around the 1 mile circuit.

START At the Forestry Commission car park at Bwlch Nant yr Arian

DIRECTIONS From Aberystwyth take the A44 towards Llangurig. Drive through Capel Bangor, Goginan and Cwmbrwyno to the sign indicating the turning left into the recreation area. There is a small parking charge or, for the impecunious, a large lay-by before the turning left.

1 From the car park descend to the visitor centre. Follow the paved path around switchbacks to the lake and path junction. Continue along the compacted gravel path by the lake. There are plenty of resting places before you reach a path junction where you will find a maker post and yellow marker. (If following the accessible walk bear right at this point and follow directions as in section 2 below). Ahead leads to a fine hide beyond a marker post. Turn right at the marker post down a rougher path and continue to another marker post. Walk straight ahead past a seat to a stile over a fence – do not cross – where you have a good view of Pond Llywernog, a man made reservoir to hold water for the nearby Llywernog lead and silver mine. This is well worth visiting after your walk. Unfortunately there is no public access to walk around this attractive stretch of water. Return along the rough path to the marker post close to the hide. Bear left and continue to the path junction. Turn left.

2 Walk alongside the lake and pass the Red Kite feeding area off to your right on a sharp left hand bend. Continue to the next path junction by the 'kite hide'. Turn left and walk easily up to a fine viewpoint of Pond Llywernog. Keep following the main path bearing right at the marker post just before the unusual 'one person seat'. Continue to the Visitor Centre and your car.

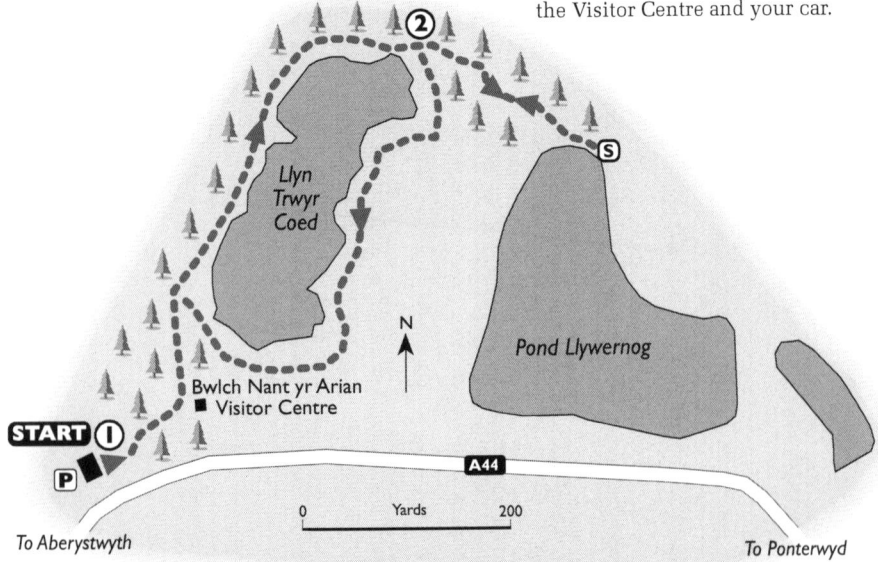

WALKS 19 & 20

WALK 20
GLASLYN

DESCRIPTION This is a very pretty stretch of water nestling high up on the very edge of the Pumlumon range. The two mile walk is further enhanced by a visit to the signed viewpoint. Views from here are breathtaking. The best months to appreciate this walk further are when the heather blooms. These are generally late July and all of August, but is a tranquil and beautiful place at any time of year. Although I have described the walk in a clockwise direction it could easily be done in the opposite one. Allow 1¼ hours.

START At the Glaslyn Reserve car park

DIRECTIONS From Machynlleth take the right turning for the mountain road off the A489 signed for Forge. Note that this road can be impassable in winter. At the summit of the road some 7½ miles from Machynlleth turn right down a gravel track where there is a sign for the Nature Reserve. Follow this track (often potholed) for a mile to where it splits. Turn up to your right, over a cattle grid, to the car parking area, where there is also an information board.

From the car park walk around the gate and follow the track to the stony lake shore. Turn left and go through a kissing gate and another 100 yards further. Follow the shoreline path – boggy in parts – to a kissing gate. Go through this and another 300 yards further. Continue along the gravel shore to a sign indicating the way to a viewpoint. This signed, grassy, but small area has outstanding views of the ravine below you, Moel Fadian with its distinctive trig point on top, Cadair Idris and the Tarrens. Return to the lake, turn left and continue your walk. Go through a gate and over a footbridge that spans the tiny outlet stream. Continue to the car park.

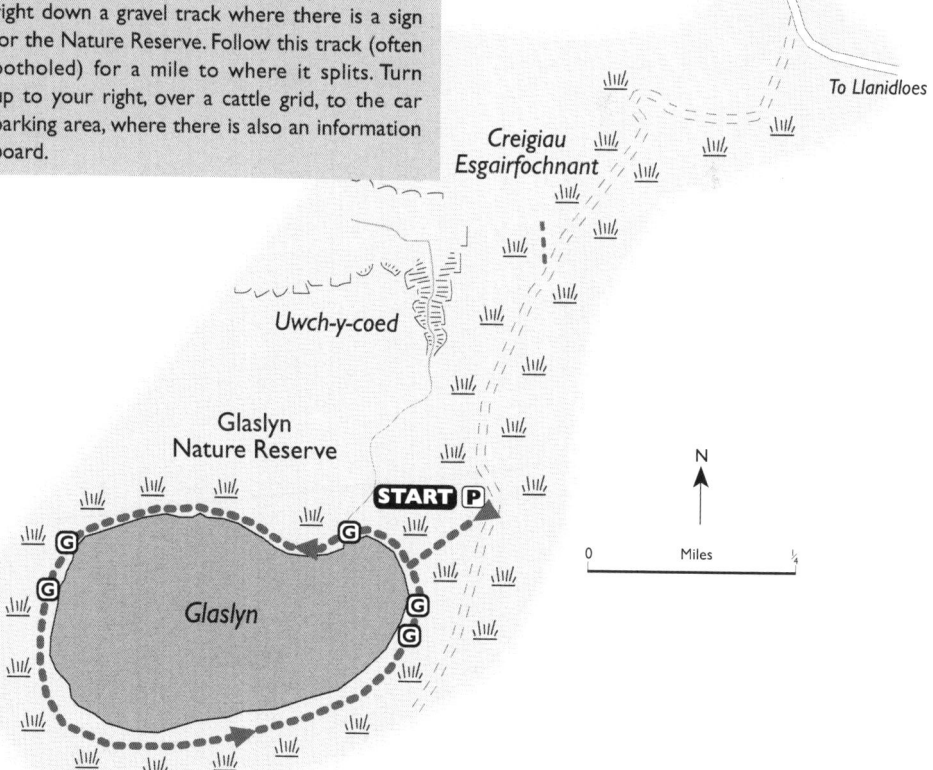

WALK 21
NANT Y MOCH

DESCRIPTION This is a challenging and very rewarding 7 miles walk with great views. The beginning and end of the walk is easy to follow but the middle section will test your route finding skills to find the easiest way.

START From the large pull in at top end of the lake on the western side.

DIRECTIONS From Aberystwyth take the A44 towards Llangurig. Go past the right turning down the A4120 for Devil's Bridge in Ponterwyd and continue along the A44 to just before the speed de-restriction sign. Turn left here onto the minor road which is signed to Nant y Moch. Follow this until level with the dam at Nant yr Moch reservoir to your left. Continue straight ahead from this junction to the dam. Before crossing it is recommended to read the information board and pay a visit to the Owen Glyndŵr memorial. At the far side of the dam turn right and follow the quiet, narrow road alongside the lake for 3¼ miles to a large pull in on your right almost opposite a stony track going up obliquely to your left. Park your car at the lower end of the lay-by allowing room for any timber trucks that occasionally turn here.

1 From your car walk up the road for 220 yards and turn right down the signed and rough no through road. Go through the gate and continue along the track to reach a stile left of a very securely locked gate. Climb over the stile. The track rises gently to reach a level section. Continue along this as it turns inland to reach a small conifer plantation. There is an abandoned farm house and a farm building. Go through the gate between the two buildings and another to your left.

2 Follow the fence on your right for 100 yards and go through a gap. Ahead is the line of a ditch. Follow the right edge of this for 330 yards to where a faint path is reached on your right – this is where the start of an examination of your route finding skills begins. Walk down this diagonally leftwards to a low swampy area. This is nowhere as bad as it looks. The path leads through it and rises slightly at the far side to reach a small area with some sloping rock. Cross this and bear left to pick up to find the path again. Contour around following intermittent paths and climb up to a grassy shoulder. Keeping at this level contour around keeping above

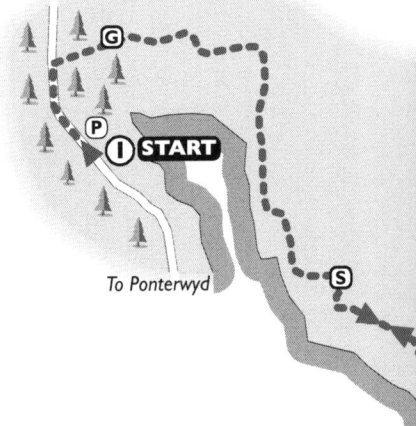

the swampy looking area below you and head towards the prominent ridge ahead. Pass by a low ruin and follow a faint path that very quickly disappears. Keep contouring and pass by a solitary old fence post. Bear diagonally left across sedges and gradually ascend to the ridge arriving just below the lowest line of low cliffs. There is also a small ruin here. Follow a faint path up and cross a low wall. *Around the ridge in front of you are great views of Nant y Moch and Hyddgen over to your left at the head of the lake.* Follow the wall to your right heading towards 4 conifers and ruins.

3 From the top edge of the ruins a faint path crosses a tiny stream and continues gradually down to reach a more distinct but narrow path. Continue along the level path before it gradually rises 30 yards above the lake and then descends almost to the shore before rising again above some rocks sticking out into the lake. On rounding the headline difficult walking through grass tussocks continues and is hard going. Eventually a better path is found close to a short section

WALK 21

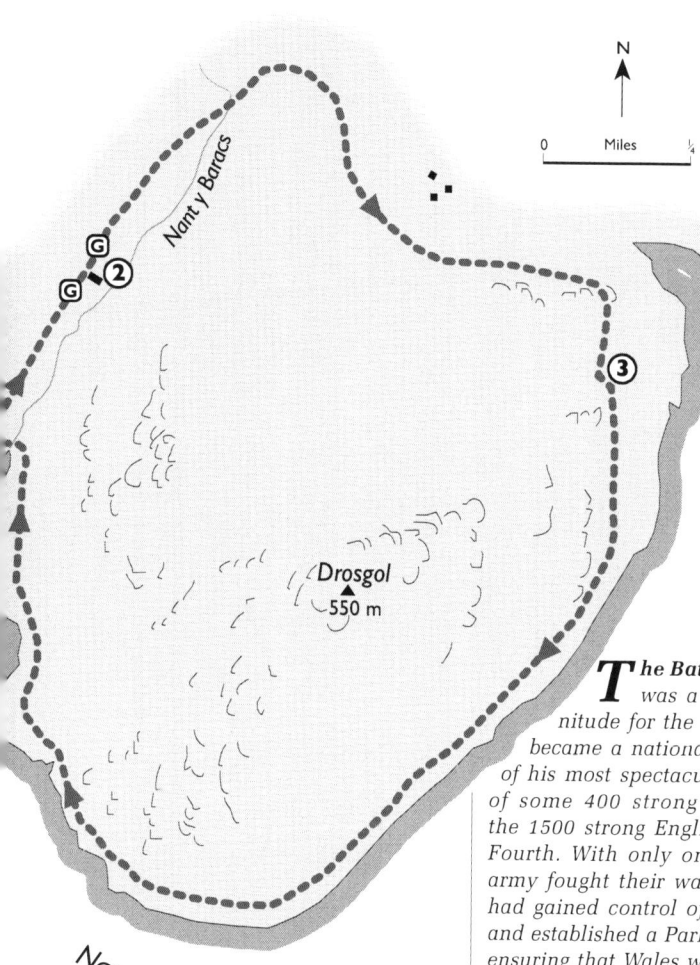

of wall. Follow it to where it ends. Drop down to cross a stream. The path is now much easier to follow and continues gradually down to the lake shore at the next inlet. Follow the shore. The level at which you do this depends on the height of the water in the lake as does the crossing of the Nant Baracas. At the far side of the stream climb steeply up to the track of your outward walk. There are now no more route finding problems. Turn left along it back to your car.

*T*he Battle of Hyddgen in 1401 was a triumph of great magnitude for the Welsh. Owain Glyndwr became a national hero as this was one of his most spectacular victories. His army of some 400 strong were surrounded by the 1500 strong English army of Henry the Fourth. With only one option left Owain's army fought their way out. By 1406 Owain had gained control of virtually all of Wales and established a Parliament in Machynlleth ensuring that Wales was a free and independent country. However, by weight of sheer numbers the English ground the Welsh down and in 1409 Owain lost most of his family when Harlech Castle fell to the despised Henry. The war ended quickly after this. In 1412 Owain was offered a free pardon by the King, but he refused this offer choosing instead to remain a fugitive. This ensured that he secured his place in history and mythology. No-one knows what happened to him after that. Some say that he died in Herefordshire in 1416 but ...... perhaps he is sleeping deep in the heart of some Welsh mountain, to wake one day to lead Wales once more.

WALK 22
LLYN GWERNAN

DESCRIPTION This 1¾ mile walk will occupy a very leisurely hour. It has really great views of Cadair Idris and its satellite peaks. The lake is a very pretty one and the walk is ideally suited for an evening when the sun highlights the cliff faces of the mountains. The walking is flat with negligible rises. There is a ¼ mile section along a quiet road. The paths used are permissive, by courtesy of the landowner, so treat them with respect.

START At the Snowdonia National Park car park, Ty Nant. Small fee payable.

DIRECTIONS From the southern end of Eldon Square in Dolgellau follow the road out of town towards Tywyn. Turn left after a ¼ mile – signed to Cadair Idris and follow this narrow, minor road for 3 miles to Ty Nant Snowdonia National Park car park on your right. Fee payable, but there are toilets here.

1 From the car park turn left onto the road and then turn left again immediately again and follow the track to a 'Y' junction. Take the right branch into the Thomas camp site. Follow the track until just past a huge pile of stones 120 yards from the junction. Cross the bottom edge of the field to reach a marker post. Beyond this two ladder stiles are seen. Walk to them and climb over the left hand one. Follow the wall on the left to another marker post. Bear left still following the wall on the left to the next marker post below a low embankment. Turn right and follow this to reach a wall which is kept on your left to pass a marker on your right. Continue to a ladder stile to the right of a gate and climb over it to another marker post. Bear left and continue through woodland to climb over another ladder stile. Follow the good path past two marker posts to a third one just before a gap in the wall. Beyond this there is a boardwalk on your right.

2 Ignore this. Continue straight ahead to reach a gate level with the end of the lake. Go through this and follow the path by the lake. There are great views of Cadair Idris from here. At a 'Y' junction of paths go right – white arrow on a marker post – to continue along the edge of the lake. Pass by a finely situated seat on your right. Just beyond this there is a small section of boardwalk that leads to a gate. Pass through this and follow the next section of boardwalk and a gravel continuation to a gate. Go through this to join a road. Turn right along this and pass the Gwernan Lake Hotel on your right

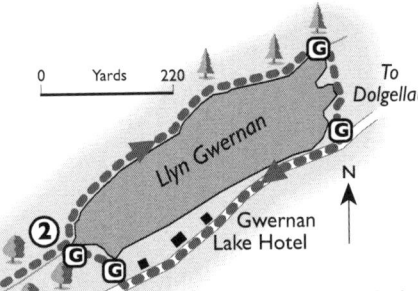

– or even have a drink before returning to your car! Continue along the road to a finger and gate on your right. Go through this and descend a short grassy slope to a boardwalk. Follow this to a marker post and turn left returning by the path you came back to the car park.

This area has been designated as a Site of Special Scientific Interest. This is due to the depth of peat found here – over 36 feet deep – which holds the complete record of pollen from plants that have grown here since the last ice age some 10,000 years ago. Because of this the disappearance of the glaciers in the area has been much more accurately dated. Juniper was one of the first trees to colonise the area followed by birch, alder and hazel trees. Very few lakes in Britain have this depth of peat.

WALK 23
LLYN Y FOEL

DESCRIPTION This is a grand 5 mile mountain walk to reach a dramatic mountain lake high on Moel Siabod. Set below the brooding summit cliffs of the mountain it becomes very mysterious in misty weather. The walk around the lake is often very boggy. Allow 3 hours.

START From the car park at Bryn Glo on the A5 in Capel Curig.

DIRECTIONS Follow the A5 from Betws y Coed towards Capel Curig. On entering the village the car park is clearly signed on you right. There is good café here for refreshment pre or post walk.

1 From the car park cross the road. Turn right and walk up the footpath, admiring the fine Cyfyng Falls on the Afon Llugwy below you on your left, to Pont Cyfyng. Go left and walk over the bridge. Continue to where a signed private road branches off to your right and a finger post indicating the way to Moel Siabod. Turn up right here and cross the cattle grid. Walk steeply up the narrow road to a sharp right hand bend. At the apex of the bend a signed path branches off to your left. Follow the gravel path up to where there are good views at the top of the rise looking towards the Carneddau. Keep on the path to join a track. Turn left up this to a house on your left.

2 Climb over the ladder stile and continue up the track to a 'Y' junction. Left goes to Rhos Quarry. Walk straight ahead up the right arm of the 'Y' and continue to reach another ladder stile. Climb over this and continue to and over the next one. The track continues to reach a very pretty un-named lake. *This has been dammed, presumably during the quar-*

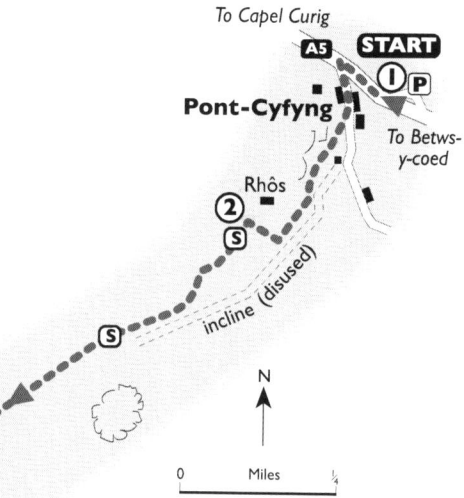

rying era. Continue up the right hand side of the lake to where the track degenerates into a rough, stony path. This rises steadily to go right around the bottom of a spoil heap and then up through the abandoned workings to a fine quarry pool. *There is often a waterfall tumbling into it.*

3 Go up left to arrive at the top of the cliff plunging into the pool. Walk across the top of the quarry and then bear left climbing steadily to suddenly view Llyn y Foel. Descend a short distance to the lake from where it is possible to walk around it on intermittent paths, though it can be boggy. *This is also a magnificent place to have lunch!* Return to your car by the same route as your ascent.

WALK 24
LLYN PADARN

DESCRIPTION This is a magnificent 5½ mile walk with much of interest, including old quarry relics, fine woodland, a bubbling stream and exceptional views. Be sure to visit the National Slate Museum either as part of your walk or afterwards to wind down! Allow 2½ hours.
START From the car park by the side of Llyn Padarn in Llanberis.
DIRECTIONS On arrival in Llanberis follow the by-pass to the obvious fee payable car park by the lake.

1 From the car park follow the path that starts next to the information board alongside the lake towards the head of it. Continue past the children's play area to enter a larger car park. Follow the path by the lake shore. Go over a footbridge and through a gate. Keep left here to follow along the lake margin guided by regular marker posts and go through another gate. *Note Dolbadarn Castle ahead.* The grassy path joins a gravel path by a footbridge. Go through the gate and cross over to reach a road. Turn left alongside the railway and follow this to pass by the National Slate Museum. Just past here turn right and cross the railway line and through a slate arch to enter Vivian Quarry. *Note the 'Blondin' cableway suspended above you, and the remarkable terracing – known as galleries – in the quarry.* Return through the arch but turn right before crossing the railway line.

2 Walk to the right of the Llanberis Lake Railway office by the sign for the V2 inclined plane and continue following red and blue ringed marker posts to this working example. From the bottom of the incline weave around the fence to walk down steps to join a path at a red ringed marker post. Follow the path up to your right to pass by a stone building on your right. When you reach the tarmac road turn left up it by a green and red ringed marker post, to pass the Visitor Centre, once the quarry hospital. Walk up the wide track to the right, marked by a green ringed marker post, passing above the Visitor Centre. Continue through a gap in the wall on the apex of a hairpin bend in the track to descend the much narrower path to a white, yellow and green ringed marker post. Walk straight ahead – *goats are often seen here* – to where the path climbs steadily. *There are great views from a balcony by a collection of signs.* Keep following the main path straight ahead going up through a fine sessile oak wood, following white and yellow ringed marker posts. *At the top of the rise there is an even better view than the previous one.* The path now descends and goes down steps to where it levels out. Pass by signs indicating the way to an old mill and continue to a gate just before a pretty stream.

3 Go through the gate and turn right. Cross the clapper bridge still following yellow and white ringed marker posts. The path ascends again and goes past a house on your left, where there is a white ringed marker post. The rest of the walk passes these from now on. A track continues through old quarry workings to pass a cottage to your right. The track becomes concrete and then tarmac as it climbs steadily to a right hand bend. Leave the track here by a marker post and walk up the short section of path to go through a gate to join a narrow road.

4 Turn left down the road and pass a phone box on your right (with no phone!). Follow the road through Fachwen to reach the end of the lake. The road bears left to reach a 'T' junction. Turn left over the

WALK 24

fine bridge – *where there are superb views of the lake and Snowdon*. Bear left at the end of the bridge to climb over a ladder stile. Continue past Craig yr Undeb to cross another ladder stile 500 yards further on the old road. Join the main road and bear left along it 150 yards to a slate 'gap' stile on your left. Go through this and descend to the bed of the old railway. Follow this easily to a barrier. Pass through the gap to the right of it and continue along a tarmac road passing toilets on your right. This road ends at the main road. Turn left along this back to your car.

Craig yr Undeb – Union Rock – was the secret meeting point for quarrymen who wanted to set up a union. The quarry owners were dead against that idea. However, in the 1870s 110 quarrymen declared themselves to be union members and were instantly locked out by Captain Wallace Cragg, the owner of Glyn Rhonway Quarry. Realising that he was losing too much money the quarrymen were reinstated three weeks later and regarded as union members. The quarry owners refused the quarrymen permission to hold meetings both in the quarries and on land owned by the estates. Lord Newborough of the Glynllifon estate allowed the men to use Craig yr Undeb. Out of these meetings the North Wales Quarrymen's Union was created.

A poem can be read at the end of the bridge over the end of the lake:

But for how?
Cherish these mountains, born in fire and ash
out of the sea to make this wilderness,
asleep for aeons beneath ice and snow,
carved by the shifting glaciers long ago,
till ten millennia back, the last ice age
made right for fern and purple saxifrage
this place whose evolution's given birth to the rare
Snowdon Lily's home on earth
but all could go with the melting snow

Gillian Clarke

39

PRONUNCIATION

These basic points should help non-Welsh speakers

Welsh	English equivalent
c	always hard, as in **c**at
ch	as on the Scottish word lo**ch**
dd	as 'th' in **th**en
f	as 'f' in o**f**
ff	as 'ff' in o**ff**
g	always hard as in **g**ot
ll	no real equivalent. It is like 'th' in **th**en, but with an 'L' sound added to it, giving 'thlan' for the pronunciation of the Welsh 'Llan'.

In Welsh the accent usually falls on the last-but-one syllable of a word.

KEY TO THE MAP

- —— Main road
- —— Minor road
- ▶ Walk route and direction
- (1) Walk instruction
- - - - Path
- ∿ River/stream
- [G] Gate
- [S] Stile
- △ Summit
- 🌲🌲 Woods
- 🍺 Pub
- (P) Parking

THE COUNTRYSIDE CODE

- Be safe – plan ahead and follow any signs
- Leave gates and property as you find them
- Protect plants and animals, and take your litter home
- Keep dogs under close control
- Consider other people

The CroW Act 2000, implemented throughout Wales in May 2005, introduced new legal rights of access for walkers to designated open country, predominantly mountain, moor, heath or down, plus all registered common land. This access can be subject to restrictions and closure for land management or safety reasons for up to 28 days a year.

Published by **Kittiwake-Books Limited**
3 Glantwymyn Village Workshops, Glantwymyn, Machynlleth, Montgomeryshire SY20 8LY

© Text & map research: Des Marshall 2013
© Maps & illustrations: Kittiwake-Books 2013
Drawings: Morag Perrott
Cover photos: *Main* – Llyn Tan-y-graig, with Cadair Idris beyond. *Inset* – Llyn Trawsfynydd. David Perrott

Care has been taken to be accurate. However neither the author nor the publisher can accept responsibility for any errors which may appear, or their consequences. If you are in any doubt about access, check before you proceed.

Printed by MWL, Pontypool.

ISBN: **978 1 908748 02 7**